KNITTING WITH BEADS

KNITTING WITH BEADS

30 BEAUTIFUL SWEATERS, SCARVES, HATS & GLOVES

JANE DAVIS

A DIVISION OF STERLING PUBLISHING CO., INC.
NEW YORK

To my loving husband,
Richard.

Editor
RONNI LUNDY

Art Direction, Design
CELIA NARANJO

Art Direction, Photo Styling
TOM METCALF
CHRIS BRYANT

Photographers
WRIGHT CREATIVE
PHOTOGRAPHY & DESIGN;
SANDRA STAMBAUGH

Cover Designer
BARBARA ZARETSKY

Illustrator
JANE DAVIS

Assistant Editor
RAIN NEWCOMB

Production Assistance
SHANNON YOKELEY
LORELEI BUCKLEY

Editorial Assistance
DELORES GOSNELL

The Library of Congress has cataloged the hardcover edition as follows:

Davis, Jane, 1959-
   Knitting with beads : 35 beautiful sweaters, scarves, hats & gloves /
by Jane Davis.
      p. cm.
   ISBN 1-57990-250-2 (hardcover)
   1. Knitting--Patterns. 2. Beadwork--Patterns. I. Title.
   TT820 .D37 2003
      746.43'20432--dc21

                                                      2002154009

10 9 8 7 6 5 4 3 2 1

Published by Lark Books, a division of
Sterling Publishing Co., Inc.
387 Park Avenue South, New York, N.Y. 10016

First Paperback Edition 2007
© 2003, Jane Davis

Distributed in Canada by Sterling Publishing,
c/o Canadian Manda Group, 165 Dufferin Street
Toronto, Ontario, Canada M6K 3H6

Distributed in the United Kingdom by GMC Distribution Services,
Castle Place, 166 High Street, Lewes, East Sussex, England BN7 1XU

Distributed in Australia by Capricorn Link (Australia) Pty Ltd.,
P.O. Box 704, Windsor, NSW 2756 Australia

The written instructions, photographs, designs, patterns, and projects in this
volume are intended for the personal use of the reader and may be reproduced
for that purpose only. Any other use, especially commercial use, is forbidden
under law without written permission of the copyright holder.

Every effort has been made to ensure that all the information in this book is
accurate. However, due to differing conditions, tools, and individual skills, the
publisher cannot be responsible for any injuries, losses, and other damages that
may result from the use of the information in this book.

If you have questions or comments about this book, please contact:
Lark Books, 67 Broadway, Asheville, NC 28801, (828) 253-0467

Manufactured in China

ISBN 13: 978-1-57990-250-6 (hardcover) 978-1-60059-135-8 (paperback)
ISBN 10: 1-57990-250-2 (hardcover) 1-60059-135-3 (paperback)

For information about custom editions, special sales, premium and corporate
purchases, please contact Sterling Special Sales Department at 800-805-5489 or
specialsales@sterlingpub.com.

CONTENTS

INTRODUCTION

 KNITTING WITH BEADS combines two fascinating, sensual processes into a craft with nearly infinite possibilities. Shining glass, warm wood, rich ceramic beads in a kaleidoscope of colors and textures can be used in so many different patterns, each a feast for the eyes and the imagination. The myriad of yarns, ranging from brilliant to oh-so-subtle color, nubby to gossamer in texture, and capable of being worked into numerous designs, make knitting equally fascinating.

My initial interest in beadwork was sparked by a project in bead knitting, the process of stringing beads on yarn before knitting, then pushing each into a stitch when needed. In 1986, I came across a magazine article on bead-knitted purses written by Alice Korach (editor-in-chief and founder of *Bead & Button* magazine). She had made a fabulous purse from an antique Berlin-work floral pattern using small, size 11 seed beads, silk thread, and size 000 steel knitting needles, so tiny they looked more like acupuncture tools. It took some 10 years and inspiration from my friend, Liz Gourley, before I actually took the time to seek the supplies (those stiletto thin needles and thread) and tried knitting with beads. It was difficult at first. I was used to pushing the tip of the needle with my finger, but had to adjust my technique so there wouldn't be a permanent hole covered with a bandage on my index finger. Once I got the hang of it, though, I was hooked. My only regret is that there isn't enough time to make all the things I want!

Designing and making the projects for this book has given me the opportunity to explore the numerous options working with beads and yarn present, and to discover the broad range of wearable items that can be created when combining the different techniques. Most published projects are either purses and bags knit with small threads, or eveningwear with bead embroidery. Although these are beautiful, knitting with beads is a much more versatile art. The results can be casual, even rustic. The sweaters, scarves, gloves, and hats you can make may be worn every day. Beads can be used as an accent along the edge of a garment, concentrated in a section with dense beadwork, or placed throughout the piece. Best of all, larger beads can be knit using thick yarn to create fresh and exciting designs—something I've concentrated on in this book. Some projects have small beads sewn onto finished knitwear, but only a few require a knitting needle smaller than size 4 and most of the needles used are much larger.

Melding beadwork with knitting is a fabulous experience, stimulating both visual and tactile senses. Mine has been a journey of discovery as I've explored ways to combine wonderful textures and vibrant hues into successful designs. With this book I hope not only to share those designs with you, but also to start you on your own journey.

GETTING STARTED

THIS BOOK COVERS SIX BASIC TECHNIQUES for knitting with beads and yarn, each presented with a number of projects using each technique. First, Beads Sewn to Knitwear features three ways to add embroidery and beadwork to finished garments. Then, Beads on the Yarn describes three methods of stringing beads onto the yarn and sliding them along the yarn as you knit. Finally, Pulling It All Together presents several projects that utilize the skills you have learned working through the projects in the first two sections by combining more than one technique in a single project.

I HAVE WRITTEN THIS BOOK for the intermediate-to-advanced knitter who may or may not have experience with beads and beadwork. The knitting instructions assume knowledge of and experience with knitting, but the beadwork instructions should be understandable even if you've never worked with beads before. Even so, experienced beadworkers who knit should enjoy this book as well, since so many of the projects use large beads, a nice break from the tiny cylinder seed beads, 15s, and charlottes that are most commonly used.

MATERIALS AND SUPPLIES

Beads

Beads come in all sizes, shapes, and colors, and are manufactured from many materials. Those used for projects in this book are made from glass, wood, clay, stone, pearl, or metal. They range from tiny size 15 seed beads embroidered on the Jeweled-Flower Sweater on page 38 to the large raku beads embroidered on the Chenille Tunic on page 48. Most projects in this book use sizes 11, 8, 6, or 5 beads. The size 11 beads are for embroidery and beadwork, the size 8 beads can be strung onto sport weight and thinner yarn, and the size 5 and 6 beads can be strung onto worsted weight yarn. Even though beads are categorized by size, you will still find that some are larger or smaller within a size, depending on the manufacturer. Also, each bead is a little different from every other bead in its lot. (Generally speaking, Japanese beads have larger threading holes and are more uniform in size.) In bead embroidery, the size of the bead you use depends only on the

look you want for the finished piece. But for the bead stringing techniques throughout this book, either the size of the bead hole, or the outside diameter of the bead, will affect the finished outcome of your project. For bead netting, beaded bands, or fringes try to use the bead sizes suggested in the project's materials list. If you need to substitute, make a small swatch of the pattern first to see if the beadwork will fit nicely when added to your knitwear. For projects in Beads on the Yarn, string some beads onto the yarn first to make sure they will fit. (Some large beads can have surprisingly small holes.) It's also a good idea to knit a small swatch to see how the bead colors look worked up in the pattern, and to see if the bead is large enough to fill the space in the design.

For projects in this book, I have listed specific bead sizes as often as possible. You may find beads like those pictured. However, in some projects you may not find nor wish to use the same beads that I used. This is your opportunity to create, and to cultivate the art of searching for that perfect bead which will express your taste.

Beads today come in many finishes, some of which are deceiving because they may appear one color, such as

blue, in a bag or tube, but will look more purple or gray when placed next to other beads or with the yarn you have chosen. Many things can affect the finished appearance of a bead: the color of thread or yarn used to sew it on; the color of the beads around it; the density of beads on the fabric. It's very disappointing to spend hours on a project only to see at the end that one of the colors was too dull, or too bright, or just not right for its place in the garment. That's why it's important to make a test swatch of your project with the beads you've selected to make sure they look the way you want them to look in the finished project.

Beads are sold in many types of containers including small plastic bags (which may be reclosable), plastic tubes, loose hanks (which are usually 12 strands of beads on thin thread), or by the individual strand. If your beads don't come in reclosable containers, you can purchase reclosable bags or use empty plastic containers to store them.

When working with beads, you need a place to put them where they won't roll all over the table and get lost on the floor. A container that will corral the beads is an important tool for beadwork and there are many types available. The simplest, least expensive, and usually the most handy is a

paper plate. Paper plates can be easily stacked for storage of a work (or many works) in progress. There are also plastic trays with separate compartments to keep bead colors organized and lids to make it easier to travel with a project you're working on.

The surface you choose to work on can also facilitate beading. There are several surfaces that beadworkers favor, such as a piece of suede, thin foam padding, or a velvet-lined board. Any of these will keep the beads from rolling and make nice surfaces for picking up the beads with a needle. You may want to try several, starting with what is on hand or easily obtainable, to find out which container and beading surface you like best.

The easiest way to pick up many beads is to have a pile of beads on your beading surface. Scoot the needle across the top of the pile so the beads slide onto the needle. Then, when the needle is full of beads, slide the beads onto the thread, counting them off by twos or fives. When you need to count a great number of beads, it helps to separate them on the yarn in groups of 100, keeping a 2- or 3-inch (5 or 7.6 cm) gap of yarn between each group. That way it's simple to count how many beads you've already strung.

Thread

Several specific thread types may be used for beadwork. A nylon continuous multifilament thread is commonly used and is readily available in many colors and sizes. It is a good choice for projects in the first three sections of the book. Silk thread is also often used, though some worry about its longevity, and it tends to tangle easily. Another popular choice is two-ply, pre-waxed, synthetic thread. For large beads, such as the wooden beads on the Carpet Bag (page 55), I use a strong cotton crochet thread or quilting thread. Try to use thread thick enough so the beadwork is not too flimsy and the beads stay in place. If you are new to beading, I encourage you to experiment with your thread choices. If you are a quilter, try quilting thread; if you crochet with thread, try that for beadwork.

Wax

Quilters and beaders alike spend a lot of time conditioning their thread so it will tangle or knot less and be easier to use. Beeswax or a special thread conditioner are common supplies in beadwork. Some threads, such as silk and cotton, benefit greatly from conditioning. To wax thread, cut the desired length, then holding it firmly against the wax or conditioner, pull the thread between your thumb and the conditioner to the end of the thread. Repeat several times so the thread is coated on both sides; then pull the thread between your fingers several times to soften the wax and help the conditioner penetrate the thread. If you are using conditioner, this will also build up static electricity in the thread so the tail will stay away from the working thread, reducing knotting.

HELPFUL TECHNIQUES

Many of the practices you have learned as a knitter will also be helpful in beadwork. There are also some techniques specific to knitting with beads that can make your work easier and the projects you produce more pleasing.

Tension

Just as in knitting, tension plays a big role in beadwork. It takes practice and experimentation to achieve the proper tension. Completing some test swatches before beginning a project can be invaluable.

When embroidering on knitwear (see Bead Embroidery, page 15), you need to be careful not to pull stitches too tight or the knitting will lose its elasticity and the beads may not stay on the front of the knitting. Then again, beads sewn too loosely on knitwear are also a problem since the thread may show or the beads may move to the back of the knitting.

However, in beadwork (see Beaded Fringe, page 15 and Beaded Applique, page 15) tension is relative. Sometimes you will want to pull all the stitches tight to make something that is sculptural, but most of the time you want your beadwork to be flexible, to fold and drape, like fabric. To achieve this effect, you must pull tight enough to get the beads to stay in place and to hide the thread, but maintain enough slack so the beadwork drapes. This is especially important for beadwork that will be attached to garments that need to drape. However, beadwork on an item such as the carpetbag will benefit from a tight stitch.

In all types of knitting with the beads pre-strung on the yarn, you need to find the proper tension so the beads stay on the front side of the knitting but don't hang low on loose strands of yarn. In knitting beads where the bead is brought in front of a slipped stitch (see Beads over Slip Stitch, page 69), you don't want to pull too tight or your knitting will be gathered along that row and the bead may slip through to the back. In Beaded Knitting (page 69), where groups of beads are draped between stitches, you need to knit tightly on either side of the beads, otherwise you will end up with a long draping strand of yarn not fully covered with beads. And finally, when doing the projects in Bead Knitting (page 99),

you need to have very tight tension so your stitches hold the beads on the front of the work.

Handling Threads in Beadwork

When we envision beadwork, we often see thousands of beads stitched together into glassy surfaces for purses and jewelry, or orderly beads worked in stitches such as peyote stitch or netting. In this type of bead-work, the goal is to have the beads organized in a specific pattern based on the thread's path through the beads. For maximum impact and sheer beauty, you will want as little of the thread to show as possible. Therefore, when weaving-in loose ends, beginning or ending a thread, always try to hide the thread in the beads, following the thread path of the stitch pattern you are using. Never pass the thread over a bead, or group of beads. And never knot where the knot, or thread, will show on the finished work.

Stitching Beads to Knitwear

When adding beads to finished knitwear, the stretch and openness of the fabric may seem to be an obstacle to getting those little beads to stay in place on the front of the garment while maintaining the fabric's elasticity. Here are two simple ways to make it easier:

1. When stitching small beads to knitted fabric, always try to stitch through a strand of yarn rather than around a knitted stitch. This way the beads are caught on the front side of the fabric and are less likely to slide around to the back of the work (see figure 1).

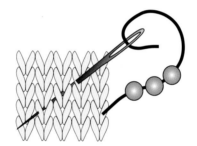

FIGURE 1

2. To preserve the horizontal stretch in a knitted fabric, either work up and down, stitching beads in place, or zigzag across the fabric. Don't make a straight horizontal line of stitching as this will eliminate the stretch in the fabric at that point (see figure 2).

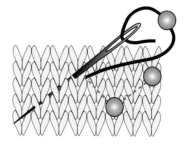

FIGURE 2

Adjusting Beadwork

Beadwork is a very personal process which, like knitting, is affected directly by how tightly or loosely each beader works her threads. A strip of beadwork done by different beaders could end up different lengths. This is because each beader has an individual "tension" when pulling the thread. Because of this, it's important to check that your beadwork will fit the intended finished knitwear item; if it won't, adjust the beadwork by completing more or fewer rows so it will fit. The same is true for embroidery and fringes where your stitching may be further apart or closer together than mine, so you will need to make more or fewer repeats of a pattern (e.g., the fringe pattern on the Fringed Autumn Shawl on page 52).

Washing Knitted Garments

Most of the projects in this book are made with hand-washable wool. I recommend spot cleaning or hand washing for most items, though a few can actually be machine washed and dried in the dryer (the Denim Tank Top on page 94 and the Striped Blouse on page 120). Treat them as you would any of your fine hand-made garments.

GLOSSARY

Backward crochet: A relatively new technique in which you work single crochet stitches toward the right, rather than the left. It creates a nice finish for knitted and crocheted garments. For details on technique, see page 96.

Bead knitting: A technique for knitting with beads in which the beads are strung onto the yarn and then pushed into stitches as the stitches are made. Traditionally made in twisted stockinette stitch in which all stitches are twisted, though projects in this book use a form of the method of plaited stockinette stitch (developed by Alice Korach) in which only the right-side stitches are twisted.

Beaded knitting: A technique of knitting with beads in which the beads are strung onto the yarn and then slid between stitches as they are made. This technique was often used for knitted purses and bags 100 years or more ago, using small beads and thread.

Cast on: Unless otherwise stated, all projects are begun with the long tail cast on method.

Double decrease (centered): Work to 2 sts before st to be decreased around. Sl the next 2 sts knitwise as one. Knit the next st. Pass the 2 sl sts over the knit st as one.

False row: There are several ways to do this. For projects in this book, the simplest way is to make a crochet chain in a contrasting yarn and pull the number of sts needed for knitting through the back loops of the chain. Later, when you are ready to knit from the "cast on" end, you simply pull out the contrasting yarn chain while inserting the knitting needle into the loops of your knitting.

Fringe: A loose or tight grouping of dangles of beads.

Netting: A variation of peyote stitch in which a group of beads are strung, and then the needle is passed through one or more beads of the row before, creating an openwork pattern.

Peyote stitch: A beadwork stitch, also known as gourd stitch, in which beads are stitched together in an offset grid pattern, like brickwork set on end, with beads being added between beads of the previous row.

Plaited stockinette stitch: On the knit row, work as for "plk," described in Abbreviations. Purl stitches are worked in the usual manner.

Reverse stockinette stitch: Wrong side of stockinette stitch used as the right side.

Stop bead: A bead tied near the end of the thread to keep beads from sliding off the thread in the beginning stages of beadwork.

ABBREVIATIONS

B#: Bead number. For beaded knitting, slide the specified number of beads up to the needle to be held in place between sts. For bead knitting, plk or purl the number of sts indicated, sliding a bead into each st as it is made.

beg: Begin/beginning.

Bp: Slide a bead into the p st.

Bplk: Slide a bead into the plk.

dec: Decrease.

dk: Double knitting, a size of yarn.

ea: Each.

inc: Increase 1 st by knitting into the back and the front of the st.

k: Knit.

k2tog: K 2 sts together as 1.

M: Make/increase one st

M1: For this increase, pick up the strand between sts and place it on the left needle. K into the back of the strand, making a new st.

M1a: Make/increase 1 st by knitting into the back of the strand after the current st.

M1b: Make/increase 1 st by knitting into the back of the strand before the current st.

M2: Make/increase 2 stitches, 1 on each side of stitch.

p: Purl.

p2tog: P 2 sts together as 1.

plk: Plaited k st: insert the right needle into the back of the st on the left needle knitwise, and wind the yarn around the right needle clockwise. Complete the st as usual.

rem: Remaining.

rtx: Right cross. Drop 2 st off the left needle. With the left needle, pick up the first st dropped, then use the right needle to pick up the second st dropped and place it on the left needle. K each st.

SKP: Slip a st, purlwise, k a st, pass the slipped stitch over the knit stitch (to dec a st).

St(s): Stitch(es).

st st: Stockinette st (k on the right side, p on the wrong side).

tog: Together.

WS: Wrong side.

yo: Yarn over.

STITCH PATTERNS

Here are instructions for two basic knitting patterns used throughout this book.

MOSS STITCH

Row 1: (k1, p1) repeat across.

Row 2: Knit the knit sts and purl the purl stitches.

Row 3: Purl the knit sts and knit the purl stitches.

To continue the pattern, repeat row 2 and row 3.

SEED STITCH

Row 1: (k1, p1) repeat across.

Row 2: Purl the knit sts and knit the purl sts.

To continue the pattern, repeat row 2.

BEADS SEWN TO KNITWEAR

In the projects in this section, beads are added to knitwear after the garment is completed. Adding beads to finished knitted items enhances the detail of the knitted design.

There are three distinct techniques in this section, bead embroidery, beaded fringe, and beadwork applique. Following are descriptions of each and, when applicable, some specific information that will help you as you make the projects. Each project is identified by a graphic that indicates which technique it employs.

BEAD EMBROIDERY

Embroidery is a vast field of needlework, which can vary from dots of detail across a surface, to densely beaded areas of color and texture. Using beads in place of colored thread and yarn adds a new texture to the surface design of the knitted garment. The projects presented here illustrate some easy ways to add beads to knitwear.

BEADED FRINGE

Beaded fringe is usually made up of long dangles of beads lined up in a row to swish, sway, and glitter as they move; but if you make them short or space them far apart you can achieve a different look altogether, as you'll see in the Chenille Tunic (page 48).

The fringe is made up of beaded strands called dangles. From two basic types of dangles, an amazing array of variations can be created by bead choice, by twisting strands of beads, and by varying the strand lengths and distance from each other.

One of the most common ways to make fringe is to string a length of beads, skip the last bead strung, and then pass the needle back up through the other beads. This creates one single hanging strand of beads with a bead at the end that holds them all in place. There are many ways to vary this basic technique. You can use different sizes of beads along the length of the strand. You can leave more than one bead at the bottom of the strand before you pass back up through the other beads. Or you can pass up through some beads, string some more beads and then pass back through some more beads, creating a thick and thin pattern in the strand.

The other type of fringe dangle is made with long, narrow loops of beads. This is the easiest and fastest type of fringe to make. Simply string the beads and then take a stitch in the fabric for each loop. The Fringed Autumn Shawl on page 52 is made with this technique.

Making beaded fringe is easy to do, but there are a few techniques you need to know in order to make it perfectly.

1. Each dangle of beads in the fringe should be pulled tightly enough so that there aren't any gaps of bare thread showing at the top of the dangles, but not so tightly that the dangles are stiff and don't drape (unless that is the intention).

2. When pulling the thread back up through the beads, hold onto the "turn around bead(s)," (the bead, or group of beads, at the bottom of each dangle that you skip before you pass the needle back up the beads). Doing this allows you to pull the other beads snugly up to the fabric.

3. It's a good idea to make a little knot after each dangle to lock the finished beadwork in place. A simple half hitch (take a small stitch in the fabric, then pass through the loop before you pull the stitch tight) is enough to hold the beads in place. Don't make a larger knot, just in case you need to correct errors.

BEADWORK APPLIQUE

These projects differ from bead embroidery in that there is a large amount of beadwork to be done and then sewn to the knitwear, as opposed to simply sewing a few beads onto the garment. This technique can be used with a variety of beadwork stitches, and has the advantage that the beadwork can, in some cases, be removable so the knitted piece can be washed separately. Be sure to review the supplies information on beads, thread, tension, and wax (page 11) if you are new to beadwork.

CABLE HAT

Here is a simple little bead embroidery detail that adds jazzy pizzazz to a classic cable hat. You can also use it on a sweater or scarf. This hat has a 2-inch-wide (5 cm) cable pattern that is repeated. The hat can be altered for a tighter or looser fit by decreasing or increasing the number of pattern repeats.

SIZE
Fits 22-in (56 cm) head

FINISHED KNITTED MEASUREMENTS
From cuff to center top: 10½ in (26.5 cm)
Turned up cuff: 3 in (7.5 cm)
Circumference: 22 in (56 cm)

MATERIAL
Approx. 220 yd (203 m), 4 oz (113 gr) of worsted-weight yarn
Approx. 10 gr of size 11 seed beads
Size 9 (5.5mm) needles or size to obtain gauge
Size 11 beading needle
Beading thread in color to match yarn and beads
Tapestry needle for sewing together seams

GAUGE IN STOCKINETTE STITCH
16 sts = 4 in (10 cm)
26 rows = 4 in (10 cm)

INSTRUCTIONS
Beginning at Brim
Cast on 122 sts.

Rows 1–30: Work the 10-st repeat in chart A 12 times, then work the last 2 sts on the chart. Repeat rows 3 to 6 five more times.
Row 31: (P2, k1, p2, k1, p2, k2) repeat to the last 2 sts, p2.
Rows 32–33: Knit the knit sts and purl the purl sts.
Row 34: K2, (p2, k2, p1, k2tog, p1, k2) repeat across (110 sts).

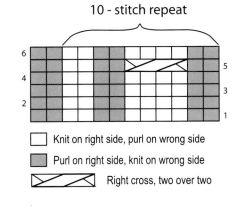

10 - stitch repeat

☐ Knit on right side, purl on wrong side

▨ Purl on right side, knit on wrong side

⬚ Right cross, two over two

CHART A

Row 35: (P2, k1, p1, k1, p2, k2) repeat to the last 2 sts, p2.

Row 36: K2, (p2, k2, p1, k1, p1, k2) repeat across.

Rows 37–40: Repeat row 35 and row 36.

Row 41: (P2, k1, p1, k1, p2, k2tog) repeat to the last 2 sts, p2 (98 sts).

Row 42: K2, (p1, k2, p1, k1, p1, k2) repeat across.

Row 43: (P2, k1, p1, k1, p2, k1) repeat to the last 2 sts, p2.

Row 44: K2, (p1, k2tog, p1, k1, p1, k2tog) repeat across (74 sts).

Row 45: (P1, k1) repeat across.

Row 46: (P1, k1, k2tog) repeat to the last 2 sts, p1, k1 (56 sts).

Row 47: P1, (k1, p2) repeat to the last st, k1.

Row 48: (P1, k2) repeat to the last 2 sts, p1, k1.

Rows 49–50: Repeat row 47 and row 48.

Row 51: (P1, k2tog) repeat to the last 2 sts, p1, k1 (38 sts)

Row 52: (P1, k1) repeat across.

Row 53: (K1, p1) repeat across.

Row 54: (K1, k2tog) repeat to the last 2 sts, k2 (26 sts).

Row 55: Purl.

Row 56: (k2tog) repeat across (13 sts).

Weave through the rem sts. Cut the tail to 24 in (61 cm) and thread with the tapestry needle. St the seam tog. Weave in ends. Turn up cuff.

Embroidery

Using the beading thread and needle, st 4 beads at the twist of each cable in one column of cables, pass the thread to the next cable along the back of the knitting, zigzagging up ½ in (1.5 cm) then down about ½ in (1.5 cm) so the hat retains its stretch. St beads to all the cables, then weave in ends.

The sample project was made using 2 skeins of Brown Sheep's Lamb's Pride, 85% wool/15% mohair, 190 yd (173 m), 4 oz (113 gr) per skein, color #115 Oatmeal.

FELTED 1920S HAT

Bead
Embroidery

SKILL LEVEL
INTERMEDIATE

*Felted knitting is a soft fuzzy fabric to which beads can be easily
sewn, creating an attractive juxtaposition of different textures.
Size is not really an issue since any bead can be sewn onto felted knitting,
and you don't have to worry much about tension and elasticity.*

MATERIALS

Approx. 250 yd (230 m) worsted-weight yarn
Size 8 (5mm) needles
Tapestry needle to sew seam
Beading thread
Beading needle
Size 11 seed beads in greens, pinks and gold

GAUGE IN STOCKINETTE STITCH BEFORE FELTING

20 sts = 4 in (10 cm)
22 rows = 4 in (10 cm)

INSTRUCTIONS

Beginning at Bottom Rim
Cast on 120 sts.

K in st st for 12 in (30 cm), ending with a knit row.

K in st st for 3 more rows, then on the next row: (k2tog, k1) repeat across. 80 sts remain.

Repeat the 4 row sequence twice more. 53 sts remain, then 32 sts remain.

P the next row.

K2tog across the next row. 16 sts remain.

Cut the yarn to about 24 in (61 cm); thread the tapestry needle, then pass through the remaining sts and stitch together the side seam. Weave in ends.

Felting

To felt the hat, put it in the washing machine with a small amount of detergent. Set on the lowest water level and hot/cold cycle, and wash.

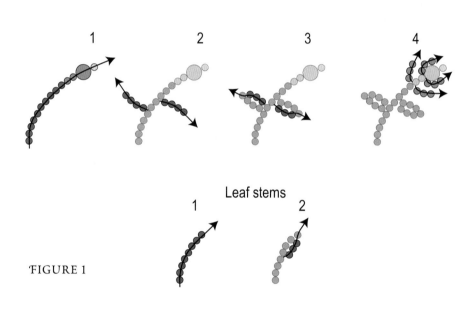

FIGURE 1

Check every five to ten minutes to see if the hat is felted small enough to fit your head. Repeat the wash cycle if necessary until the hat is the proper size. Turn up the edges of the hat, forming it to your desired shape, then let the hat dry overnight in a warm place.

Embroidery

To sew the flowers on the hat, follow the steps in figure 1, using the photo of the hat on page 19 for placement.

Sew leaf stems and flower stems along the front of the hat about 1½ to 2 in (4 to 5 cm) from the rim. Dot gold beads among the greenery by stitching a single gold bead here and there. Weave in ends.

The sample project was made using one 8-ply Wool Pak of Baabajoes yarn, 100% wool, 525 yd (485 m), 7 oz (250 gr) per skein, color #35 Aubergine.

FAIR ISLE VEST

If you like knitting in colorwork, here is a fun vest with easy bead embroidery in backstitch duplicating the Fair Isle pattern. Because the vest is loose and doesn't need to stretch to fit, the bead embroidery can be stitched horizontally across the knitting. Be careful not to pull the stitches too tight though or you may distort the vest.

SIZES

To fit chest sizes 34 in (36, 38, 40, 42 in), (86.5, 91.5, 96.5, 101.5, 106.5 cm). Instructions are for the smallest size, with larger sizes in parentheses. If there are no parentheses, the number is for all sizes.

FINISHED KNITTED MEASUREMENTS

Bust: 36 in (38, 40, 42, 44 in), (91.5, 96.5, 101.5, 106.5, 112 cm)
Length: 21½ in (22, 22½, 23, 23½ in), (54.5, 56, 57, 58.5, 59.5 cm)

MATERIALS

8 (9, 9, 10, 11) 126 yd (115 m) skeins of sport-weight yarn in plum
2 skeins each in burgundy, teal, and sky blue
1 skein each in pale green and forest green
Size 3 (3.25 mm) and 4 (3.5 mm) knitting needles or size to obtain gauge
Medium tapestry needle with an eye large enough to thread the yarn, and thin enough to string the beads
Less than 1 oz (28 gr) each of size 6 beads to match the burgundy, teal, plum, and forest green yarns

GAUGE IN STOCKINETTE STITCH USING THE SIZE 4 NEEDLES

6 sts = 1 in (2.5 cm)
7 rows = 1 in (2.5 cm)

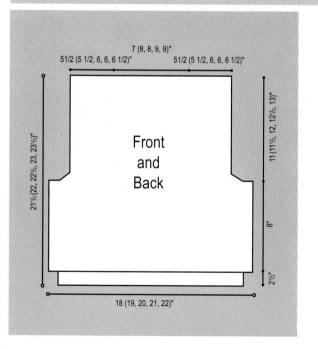

Front and Back

7 (8, 8, 9, 9)"
5 1/2 (5 1/2, 6, 6, 6 1/2)"   5 1/2 (5 1/2, 6, 6, 6 1/2)"
11 (11½, 12, 12½, 13)"
21½ (22, 22½, 23, 23½)"
8"
2½"
18 (19, 20, 21, 22)"

■ Plum
■ Burgundy
□ Pale yellow green
□ Sky blue
■ Green
■ Forest green

CHART A

INSTRUCTIONS

Back of Vest

Using the size 3 (3.25 mm) needles, cast on 107 (113, 119, 125, 131) sts.

Rows 1–4: (k1, p1) repeat across to the last stitch, k1.
Row 5: K2, (yo, k2tog, k1) repeat across.
Row 6 and all even rows: (p2, k1) repeat to the last 2 sts, p2.
Rows 7, 9, 17, 19, and 21: (k2, p1) repeat to the last 2 sts, k2.
Rows 11, 13 and 15: K2, p1 (rtx, p1) repeat to the last 2 sts, k2.

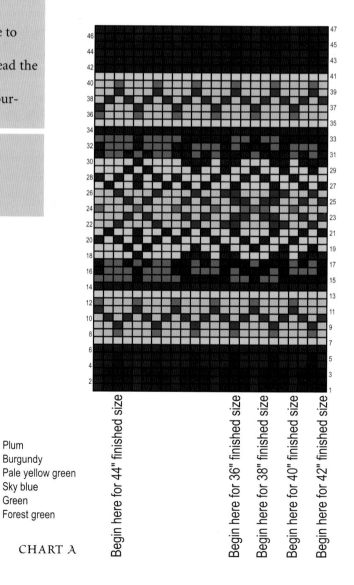

Begin here for 44" finished size

Begin here for 36" finished size

Begin here for 38" finished size

Begin here for 40" finished size

Begin here for 42" finished size

Change to size 4 (3.5 mm) needles and work in st st until the vest measures 10½ in (26.5 cm) from the bottom edge.

Decrease at sides for armholes as follows: Bind off 4 sts at the beg of the next 2 rows, 99 (105, 111, 117, 123) sts. Decrease 1 st at each side on every other row, 3 times, 93 (99, 105, 111, 117) sts. Begin colorwork pattern, following chart A. Work even in pattern, then 3 in (3½, 4, 4½, 5 in), (7.5, 9, 10, 11.5, 12.5 cm) more in plum, in st st. Bind off loosely.

Front of Vest
Knit the same as for back.

Assembly and Armholes
Sew shoulder and side seams together. Using size 4 (3.5 mm) needles, pick up 122 (128, 134, 140, 144) sts around one armhole and knit in reverse stockinette for 6 rows. Bind off. Roll reverse stockinette band around selvage of armhole and sew in place, covering selvage edge. Repeat for other armhole. Turn up bottom edge of ribbing at Row 5, stitch in place to back of ribbing.

Embroidery

Attach a 24-in (61 cm) length of plum yarn to the top right front of the large repeat of colorwork pattern. String a bead, and backstitch to the next plum stitch on the same row

This bead embroidery technique can be used on any knitwear pattern, including store-bought items you may wish to enhance with beadwork. It's easy to follow the color pattern, stitching the beads in place. You could also make up your own pattern and, as you would do for cross-stitch, simply sew on the beads using the knit stitches as a canvas. Since knitting isn't square, if you use a design on a square graph, such as a cross-stitch pattern, the finished design on the knitwear will be distorted a bit. However, with floral and abstract designs this usually isn't a disadvantage.

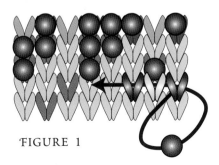

FIGURE 1

(see figure 1). Repeat across the row, and for each row of the large repeat pattern, covering the foreground pattern, using a yarn color similar to the beads. Add 1 row of beads in the same way across the smaller repeat patterns, except stitch contrasting color beads to add to the design.

The sample project was made using Dale of Norway Tiur, 60% mohair/40% new wool, 8 (9, 9, 10, 11) 1.75 oz (50 gr), 126 yd (115 m) skeins in plum #5172, 2 skeins each in burgundy #4155, teal #7053, and sky blue # 6222, and 1 skein each in pale green # 8533 and forest green # 7562.

CABLE COAT

*This cozy coat knits up quickly with thick,
color-flecked, single-ply yarn and big needles.
The bead embroidery adds an elegant finishing detail,
blending in with the yarn color yet adding another texture to the cable and seed stitch pattern.*

SIZES

To fit chest sizes 34 in (36, 38, 40, 42 in), (86.5, 91.5, 96.5, 101.5, 106.5 cm).
Instructions are for the smallest size with larger sizes in parentheses. If
there are no parentheses, the number is for all sizes.

FINISHED MEASUREMENT

Bust: 40 in (42, 44, 46, 48 in), (101.5, 106.5, 111.5, 117, 122 cm)
Length: 24 in (25, 26, 27, 28 in), (62, 63.5, 66, 68.5, 71 cm)
Upper Arm: 17 in (17, 17½, 18, 18 in), (43, 43, 44.5, 45.5, 45.5 cm)

MATERIALS

Approx. 12 (13, 13, 14, 15) 110 yd (101 m) skeins of heavy-weight yarn
Size 11.5 (8.5 mm) needles, or size to obtain gauge
Approx. 1.75 oz (49 g) size 11 seed beads
Approx. 1.5 oz (42 g) size 8 seed beads
Approx. 1.25 oz (35 g) rectangular beads or niblets
Size 11 beading needle
Sewing thread
4 buttons, 1 in diameter
Optional: ½- to ¾-inch-thick (1 to 2 cm) shoulder pads
Tapestry needle for sewing together seams

GAUGE IN STOCKINETTE STITCH

14 sts = 4 in (10 cm)
19 rows = 4 in (10 cm)
Pattern repeat from chart A = 7½ in (19 cm) wide

INSTRUCTIONS

Back

Cast on 64 (68, 72, 76, 80) sts. Beginning where indicated for size, repeat pattern in chart A 3 times then pattern in chart B (except for smallest size), until back measures 15 in (15½, 16, 16½, 17 in), (38, 39.5, 40.5, 42, 43 cm). Cast off 4 sts at the beg of the next two rows. Dec 1 st at ea end every right side row, 4 times, 48 (52, 56, 60, 64) sts. Work even in pattern until back measures 24 in (25, 26, 27, 28 in), (61, 63.5, 66, 68.5, 71 cm). Bind off.

Right Front

Cast on 34 (36, 38, 40, 42) sts. Work pattern from chart C for 17 rows.

Buttonhole

Beginning on right side, work 3 rows in first 3 sts in pattern. Break off yarn. Begin yarn at fourth st on right side and work 3 rows of remaining sts in pattern. Beginning on the wrong side, work across all sts.

Work in pattern making buttonholes 14(14, 15, 15, 16) rows apart, continuing in pattern until the front measures 15 in (15½, 16, 16½, 17 in), (38, 39.5, 40.5, 42, 43 cm). Beginning on a wrong-side row, cast off 4 sts at the side seam. On the next 4 right-side rows, dec 1 st at the side seam. At the same time, increase 1 st every fourth row at the * on the pattern (this creates the lapel) 3(3, 4, 4, 4) times, 29 (31, 34, 36, 38) sts, working the additional stitches in seed stitch.

Continue in pattern until the piece measures 22 in (23, 24, 25, 26 in), (56, 58, 61, 63.5, 66 cm). Beginning on a right-side row, cast off the first 7(7, 8, 8, 8) sts (the top of the lapel) continuing in pattern across the row,

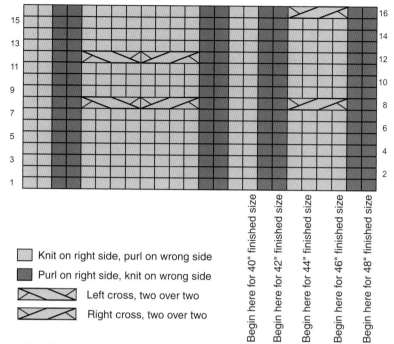

Knit on right side, purl on wrong side

Purl on right side, knit on wrong side

Left cross, two over two

Right cross, two over two

Begin here for 40" finished size
Begin here for 42" finished size
Begin here for 44" finished size
Begin here for 46" finished size
Begin here for 48" finished size

CHART A

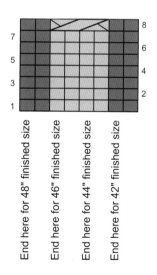

End here for 48" finished size
End here for 46" finished size
End here for 44" finished size
End here for 42" finished size

Knit on right side, purl on wrong side

Purl on right side, knit on wrong side

Right cross, two over two

CHART B

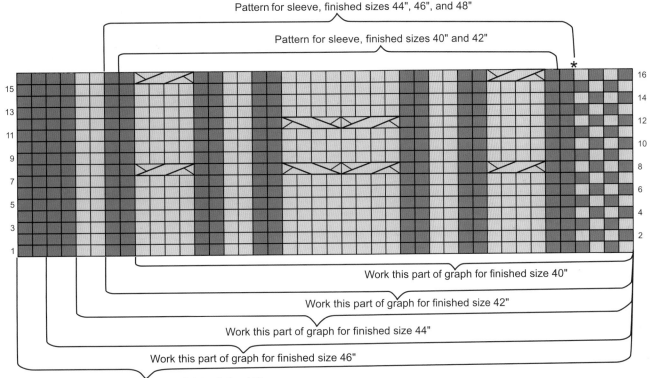

Pattern for sleeve, finished sizes 44", 46", and 48"

Pattern for sleeve, finished sizes 40" and 42"

Work this part of graph for finished size 40"

Work this part of graph for finished size 42"

Work this part of graph for finished size 44"

Work this part of graph for finished size 46"

Work this part of graph for finished size 48"

CHART C

☐ Knit on right side, purl on wrong side

■ Purl on right side, knit on wrong side

Left cross, two over two

Right cross, two over two

22 (24, 26, 28, 30) sts. Continuing in pattern, decrease 1 st at center front ea right-side row, 3 times 19 (21, 23, 25, 27) sts. Continue in pattern until piece measures 24 in (25, 26, 27, 28 in), (61, 63.5, 66, 68.5, 71 cm). Bind off.

Left Front
Cast on 34 (36, 38, 40, 42) sts. Work pattern from chart D until the front measures 15 in (15½, 16, 16½, 17 in), (38, 39.5, 40.5, 42, 43 cm). Beginning on a right side row, cast off 4 sts at the side seam. On the next 4 right-side rows, dec 1 st at the side seam. At the same time, increase 1 st every fourth row at the * on the pattern

(this creates the lapel) 3 (3, 4, 4, 4) times, 29 (31, 34, 36, 38) sts.

Continue in pattern until the piece measures 22 in (23, 24, 25, 26 in), (56, 58, 61, 63.5, 66 cm). Beginning on a wrong-side row, cast off the first 7 (7, 8, 8, 8) sts (the top of the lapel) continuing in pattern across the row, 22 (24, 26, 28, 30) sts. Continuing in pattern, decrease 1 st at center front ea right-side row, 3 times 19 (21, 23, 25, 27) sts. Continue in pattern until piece measures 24 in (25, 26, 27, 28 in), (61, 63.5, 66, 68.5, 71 cm). Cast off.

Sleeve
Cast on 30 (30, 30, 32, 32) sts. Work in pattern following section indicated in chart C, increasing 1 st ea side every 4 rows 12 (12, 13, 13, 13) times, 54 (54, 56, 58, 58) sts. Work increased stitches in seed stitch. Work even until sleeve measures 14 in (14½, 14½, 15, 15 in), (35.5, 37, 37, 38, 38 cm). Cast off 4 sts at the beginning of the next 2 rows, 46 (46, 48, 50, 50) sts. Decrease 1 st ea side every other row 4 times, 38 (38, 40, 42, 42) sts. Decrease 1 st ea side every 6 (6, 7, 7, 8) rows, 3 times, 32 (32, 34, 36, 36) sts. Decrease 1 st ea side every other row 3 (3, 3, 4, 4)

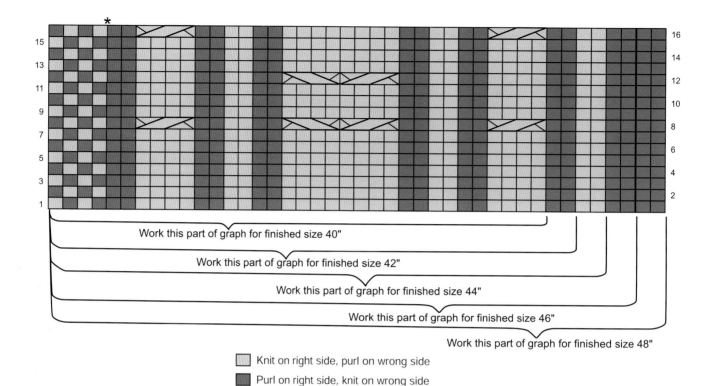

Work this part of graph for finished size 40"

Work this part of graph for finished size 42"

Work this part of graph for finished size 44"

Work this part of graph for finished size 46"

Work this part of graph for finished size 48"

Knit on right side, purl on wrong side

Purl on right side, knit on wrong side

Left cross, two over two

Right cross, two over two

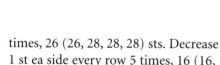

CHART D

times, 26 (26, 28, 28, 28) sts. Decrease 1 st ea side every row 5 times, 16 (16, 18, 18, 18) sts. Bind off.

Block all pieces.

Beadwork
Beginning with the back of the coat, attach a 6-foot (1.8 m) length of beading thread to the bottom of one of the k2 ribs on either side of the large center cable. String 2 size 11 seed beads, 1 size 8 seed bead, 1 rectangular bead, 1 size 8 seed bead, and 2 size 11 seed beads. Stitch through the third row above, as shown in photo. Repeat this pattern to the top

of the rib. Stitch beads in the same pattern to the rib on the other side of the large cable. Repeat for the left and right front pieces and the sleeves.

Assembly
Stitch the shoulder seams together. Stitch the sleeves in place, then the side and sleeve seams. If desired, leave a 3-in (7.5 cm) slit at the bottom of the side seams.

Collar
Beginning at the center side of the right front, at the right corner of the top of the lapel, pick up 7 sts along

the right front, 11 (11, 14, 14, 14) sts along the back, and 7 sts along the left front. Knit in seed st for 7 (7, 8, 8, 8) rows. Bind off.

Finishing
Weave in ends. Sew buttons to left front band opposite button holes on right front band. (Optional: stitch shoulder pads along shoulder seams.)

The sample project was made using 13 skeins of Reynolds Lopi 100% virgin wool, 3.5 oz (100 gr), 110 yd (10 m) in denim #0735.

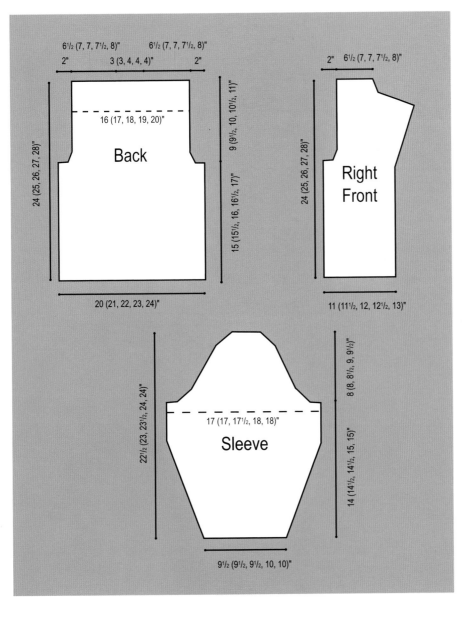

Back

6½ (7, 7, 7½, 8)"   6½ (7, 7, 7½, 8)"

2"   3 (3, 4, 4, 4)"   2"

16 (17, 18, 19, 20)"

24 (25, 26, 27, 28)"

9 (9½, 10, 10½, 11)"

15 (15½, 16, 16½, 17)"

20 (21, 22, 23, 24)"

Right Front

2"   6½ (7, 7, 7½, 8)"

24 (25, 26, 27, 28)"

11 (11½, 12, 12½, 13)"

Sleeve

22½ (23, 23½, 24, 24)"

17 (17, 17½, 18, 18)"

8 (8, 8½, 9, 9½)"

14 (14½, 14½, 15, 15)"

9½ (9½, 9½, 10, 10)"

RUSTIC SWEATER

Because the knitting is not blocked, this cozy, thick, wool sweater has extra loft and maintains the dense texture of the ribbing and cables. The addition of embroidered wooden beads along the sleeves and yoke adds to the rustic look of the tweed green yarns.

SIZES

To fit chest sizes 34 in (36, 38, 40, 42 in), (86.5, 91.5, 96.5, 101.5,106.5 cm). Instructions are for the smallest size, with larger sizes in parentheses. If there are no parentheses, the number is for all sizes.

FINISHED KNITTED MEASUREMENTS

Bust: 36 in (38, 40, 42, 44 in), (91.5, 96.5, 101.5, 106.5, 110.5 cm)
Length: 17½ in (17½, 18.18.18 ½in), (44.5, 44.5, 45.5, 45.5 cm, 47 cm)
Upper Arm: 18½ in (18½, 19. 19, 19½ in), (47, 47, 48.5, 48.5 cm, 49.5 cm)

MATERIALS

Approx. 366 yd (329 m) each of worsted-weight yarn in 6 shades of the same color
Approx. 325 6mm round wooden beads
Size 10½ (6 mm) needles, or size to obtain gauge, for front and back of sweater
Size 9 (5.25 mm) needles or size to obtain gauge, for sleeve and yoke of sweater
Size 11 beading needle
Sewing thread
Tapestry needle for sewing together seams

GAUGE IN STOCKINETTE STITCH USING SIZE 10½ (6 MM) NEEDLES AND HOLDING TWO STRANDS OF YARN TOGETHER AS ONE

14 sts = 4 in (10 cm)
18 rows = 4 in (10 cm)
Gauge in stockinette stitch using size 9 (5.5 mm) needles and holding two strands of yarn together as one
16 sts = 4 in (10 cm)
20 rows = 4 in (10 cm)

INSTRUCTIONS

Back

Using size 10½ (6 mm) needles with 2 strands of the darkest color yarn, cast on 74 (78, 82, 86, 90) sts. Work in pattern from chart A, changing 1 strand of yarn to the next lighter color every sixth row. On the eleventh color sequence (two strands of the lightest color) work in those colors until the back measures 13½ in (13¾, 14, 14½, 15 in), (34.5, 35, 35.5, 37, 38 cm). Bind off.

Front

Work the same as the back.

Sleeve and Yoke

Using size 9 (5.25 mm) needles and holding 2 strands of the darkest color yarn as 1, cast on 32 (32, 34, 34, 36) sts. Work in pattern from chart B, changing 1 strand of yarn to the next lighter color every ninth row, increasing 1 st ea side in pattern every third row, 24 times, 80 (80, 82, 82, 84) sts. Work even in pattern and continuing color changes until sleeve measures 17½ in (17½, 18, 18, 18½ in), (44.5, 44.5, 45.5, 45.5, 47 cm). Bind off 6 sts at the beg of the next 2 rows. Work even for 4½ in (4½, 4½, 4¾, 4¾ in), (11.5, 11.5, 11.5, 12, 12 cm). Bind off center 8 sts. Working each side separately, work even for 3¾ in (4, 4¼, 4¼, 4¼, 4½ in) (9.5, 11, 11, 11, 11.5 cm). Move sts to st holders. Repeat for the other sleeve and yoke.

Assembly

Graft together the center front of yoke pieces and the center back yoke pieces. Stitch sleeve seams together. Stitch side seams of front and back together, leaving a 3-in (7.5-cm) slit at the bottom of the side seams, if desired. Stitch the front and back to the yoke and sleeve.

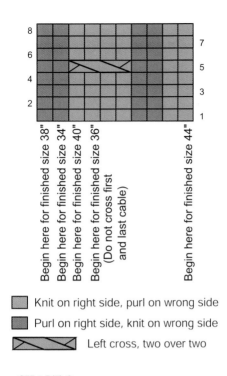

Begin here for finished size 38"
Begin here for finished size 34"
Begin here for finished size 40"
Begin here for finished size 36" (Do not cross first and last cable)
Begin here for finished size 44"

▨ Knit on right side, purl on wrong side
▨ Purl on right side, knit on wrong side
⬳ Left cross, two over two

CHART A

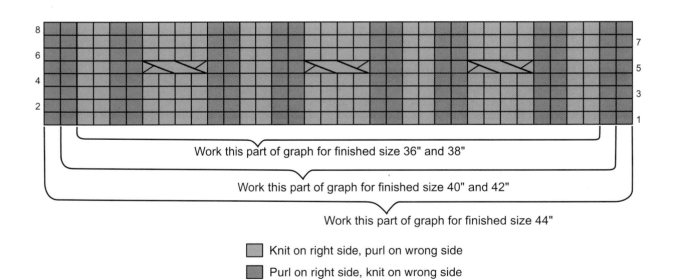

Work this part of graph for finished size 36" and 38"

Work this part of graph for finished size 40" and 42"

Work this part of graph for finished size 44"

▨ Knit on right side, purl on wrong side
▨ Purl on right side, knit on wrong side
⬳ Left cross, two over two

CHART B

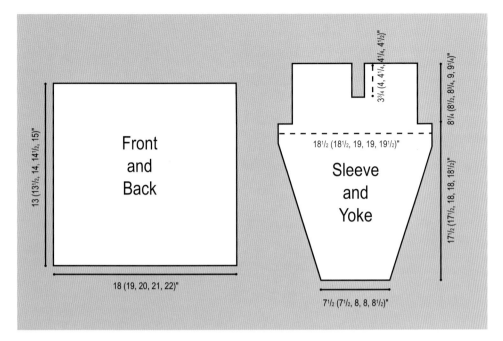

Front
and
Back

13 (13½, 14, 14½, 15)"

18 (19, 20, 21, 22)"

Sleeve
and
Yoke

3¾ (4, 4½, 4¼, 4½)"

18½ (18½, 19, 19, 19½)"

8¼ (8½, 8¾, 9, 9¼)"

17½ (17½, 18, 18, 18½)"

7½ (7½, 8, 8, 8½)"

Embroidery

Using the sewing thread doubled for strength, stitch 1 bead between each cable twist along the 3 center cables of the sleeve and yoke. Then stitch 1 bead every fourth row along the 4 purl strips between the 3 cables.

This project was made using Tahki Yarns Donegal Tweed, 100% pure new wool, 3.5 oz (100g), 183 yd (169 m), 2 skeins each of dark green #849, forest green # 878, medium green # 807, grass green # 803, yellow green # 855, and pale green # 825.

FELTED FALL VEST

Felting makes a great fabric for beadwork. It's easy to embroider on felted knitting and the fuzzy texture of the dense yarn makes a wonderful backdrop, contrasting with the sparkling surface of the beads. Here large hexagonal beads shine against a green trellis pattern, and semi-precious stone bead leaves shimmer among bead acorns, flowers, and berries, all worked in an autumn color scheme.

INSTRUCTIONS

Cast on 200 (210, 220, 230, 240) sts. Join into a circle. Place marker.

Knit rows 1 through 5 of chart A.

Knit 7 repeats of rows 6 through 21 of chart A.

Knit rows 22 through 24 of chart A.

Flatten tube so design is symmetrical on both sides of center front. Graft tog shoulders at top.

Sew bottom tog loosely with white pearl cotton (remove after felting).

Felting
To felt the vest, put it in the washing machine on the lowest water level and hot/cold cycle, with a small amount of detergent. Check every five to ten minutes to see if the vest is felted. Repeat the wash cycle if necessary until the vest is the desired size. Dry flat overnight in a warm place.

Finishing and Embroidery
Follow the schematic to cut the center front opening and armholes.

SIZES
To fit chest sizes 34 in (36, 38, 40, 42 in), (86. 5, 91.5, 96.5, 101.5, 106.5 cm). Instructions are for the smallest size, with larger sizes in parentheses. If there are no parentheses, the number is for all sizes.

FINISHED MEASUREMENTS
Bust: 36 in (38, 40, 42, 44 in), (91.5, 96.5, 101.5, 106.5, 111.5 cm)
Length: 20 in (21, 22, 22, 23 in), (51, 53, 56, 56, 58 cm)

MATERIALS
Approx. 390 yd (351 m) each of dk-weight yarn in forest green and gold
Size 9 (5.5 mm) circular needle, or size to obtain gauge
Stitch marker
Approx. 2 oz of large hexagonal beads
Ten ¾-inch-long (2 cm) leaf beads
Approx. 30 small ½-in (1 cm) leaf beads in two or more shapes and colors
Approx. ½ oz (14 gr) dark green size 11 seed beads
Various odd-shaped beads in greens and golds
Size 11 beading needle
Beading thread
Tapestry needle for sewing together seams
Hand-sewing needle and matching thread to sew edging to vest
White pearl cotton to baste bottom edges tog before felting
(Optional: ¾ yd [.7 m] lining fabric, matching thread)

GAUGE IN STOCKINETTE STITCH BEFORE FELTING
17 sts = 4 in (10 cm)
20 rows = 4 in (10 cm)

Back stitch the hexagonal beads at each point where the green lines cross on the knit pattern.

Using a variety of leaf and other beads, make a collection of fall images by sewing beads on the bottom sections of the vest, as shown in figure 1.

Step 1: Stitch the largest leaf beads, outlining the shape of the overall embroidery.

Step 2: Sew on the smaller leaves, stitching several size 11 seed beads for stems. Make flowers and acorns out of any odd-shaped beads available.

Step 3: Use the size 11 seed beads to fill in with leaves made of a center strand of beads with shorter strands forming the leaf shape. Add any medium beads in groups for clusters of berries.

If you want to add a lining, fold the lining fabric inside the vest, wrong sides together so the fabric selvage edges are at the opening of the vest, and the top raw edges of the fabric overlap at least 1 in (2.5 cm) at the shoulder. Pin the lining in place along the edges of the vest. Allow ½ in (1.5 cm) shoulder seams in the lining, and turn under so they meet at the shoulder line. Cut the rest of the lining ½ in (1.5 cm) beyond the bottom of the vest and flush with the arm hole and center front and neck opening. Turn up the bottom edge of the lining and stitch to the vest. Stitch the shoulder seams, and baste the remaining edges of lining close to the edge of the vest.

Using the green yarn, knit a 6-st-wide band in st st long enough to go around all the raw edges of the vest (approx. 120 in [305 cm]). With right sides tog, using sewing thread

to match the green, sew the band to the cut edges about ⅜ in (9.5 mm) from the raw edges. Begin at the bottom of one side of the front, around the neckline, and down the second side of the front of the vest. Cut the band about ½ in (1.5 cm) beyond where you finish, unravel the end and weave into the vest. Attach the same way for the armholes, grafting the ends together at the bottom of the armhole. Stretch the band a little as you sew it along the bottom arm-hole edges and neckline so it will lay flat when folded over. Fold over to the inside and sew in place, covering the raw edges of the lining, if using a lining.

The sample project was made using one Wool Pak each of Baabajoes 10-ply yarn, 100% wool, 9 oz (250 gr), 430 yd (396 m) in goldstone #27 and forest #12.

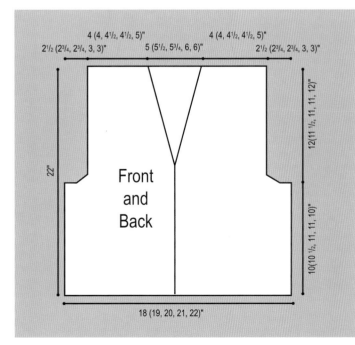

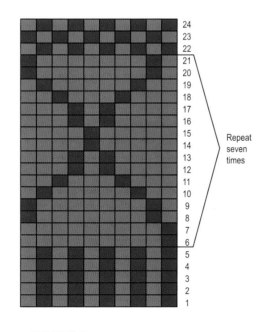

CHART A

1

2

3

FIGURE 1

JEWELED‑FLOWER SWEATER

Bead Embroidery

SKILL LEVEL
INTERMEDIATE

In this sweater, the pattern is worked up in fall colors, but it would be equally stunning in white cotton with pale or bright spring flowers, or black background yarn with jewel-tone or Christmas-colored flowers.

INSTRUCTIONS

Back

Cast on 76 (80, 84, 88, 94) sts. Work in k1, p1 rib for 2½ in (6.5 cm). Work in st st until piece measures 17½ in (18½, 19½, 19½, 20½ in), (44.5, 47, 49.5, 49.5, 52 cm). Set aside. Cast on 76 (80, 84, 88, 94) sts and make k1, p1 rib 2½ in (6.5 cm) long. Graft ribbing to top of back. Weave in ends.

Front

Cast on 76 (80, 84, 88, 94) sts. Work k1, p1 rib for 2½ in (6.5 cm). End on wrong side row. Beg pattern as follows. Knit 11 (13, 15, 17, 20) sts in oatmeal then follow chart A, repeating 3 times, then follow chart B, then knit last 11 (13, 15, 17, 20) sts of row in oatmeal. Repeat pattern in st st until front measures 17½ in (18½, 19½, 19½, 20½in), (44.5, 47, 49.5, 49.5 cm, 52 cm). Set aside. Cast on 76 (80, 84, 88, 94) sts and make k1, p1 rib 2½ in (6.5 cm) long. Graft ribbing to top of front. Weave in ends.

SIZES

To fit chest sizes 34 in (36, 38, 40, 42 in), (86.5, 91.5, 96.5, 101.5, 106.5 cm). Instructions are for the smallest size, with larger sizes in parentheses. If there are no parentheses, the number is for all sizes.

FINISHED KNITTED MEASUREMENTS

Bust: 36 in (38, 40, 42, 44 in), (91.5, 96.5, 101.5, 106.5, 111.5 cm)
Length: 20 in (21, 22, 22, 23 in), (51, 53.5, 56, 56, 58. cm)
Upper Arm: 16 in (16, 16½, 17, 17 in), (40.5, 40.5, 42, 43 cm, 43 cm)

MATERIALS

6 (6, 6, 7, 7) 190 yd (140 m) skeins of worsted-weight yarn in oatmeal
One 172 yd (164 m) skein of worsted-weight yarn in green
Approx. ½ oz (14 gr) of size 11 and size 15 seed beads in green and golds for the stems
Various odd-shaped beads of glass, stone, or gems for the flowers
Size 9 (5.25 mm) needles, or size to obtain gauge
Size 11 beading needle
Beading thread
Tapestry needle for sewing together seams

GAUGE IN STOCKINETTE STITCH

4.25 sts = 1 in (2.5 cm)
5 rows = 1 in (2.5 cm)

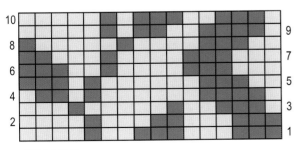

CHART A

Oatmeal
Green

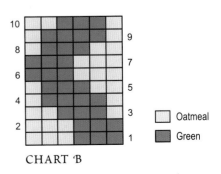

CHART B

Oatmeal
Green

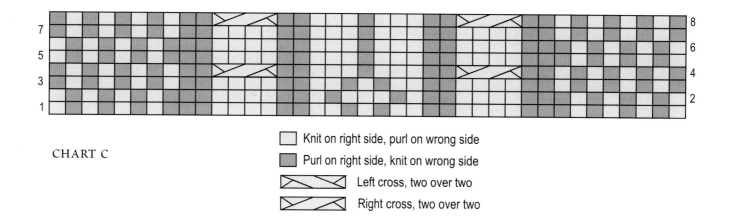

CHART C

☐ Knit on right side, purl on wrong side

▨ Purl on right side, knit on wrong side

⬗ Left cross, two over two

⬗ Right cross, two over two

Note: Chart C is for smallest size. For larger sizes, center design and work extra sts on sides in moss pattern.

Sleeves

Beginning at cuff, cast on 39 (39, 41, 43, 43) sts. Work in st st for 8 rows, then follow pattern in chart C, increasing 1 st in pattern at ea end every fifth row 14 times (67, 67, 69, 71, 71) sts). Work even in pattern until sleeve measures 17½ in (18, 18½, 19, 19½ in), (44.5 , 45.5, 47, 48.5, 49.5 cm) from rolled cuff. Bind off.

Gore

Cast on 10 sts. Working in moss st, dec 1 stitch at ea end on the third, ninth, nineteenth, and twenty-seventh row, knit 2 more rows. Bind off.

Finishing and Embroidery

Block all pieces to measurements. Embroider bead flowers to knitted vines, choosing patterns from the eight flower designs in figure 1, or creating your own. Tack front and back together at top corners. Center top of sleeve where front and back are tacked tog, and sew sleeve top to front and back. Sew side seams of sleeves and body. Sew gores in place under front and back edges.

The sample project was made using 6 skeins of Lamb's Pride Worsted, 85% wool/15% mohair, 190 yd (173m), 4 oz (113 gr) per skein, in color #115 Oatmeal by Brown Sheep Company, and 1 skein of Harmony, 100% wool, 172 yd (155 m), 4 oz (112 gr) per skein in color #9 olive by Reynolds Yarns.

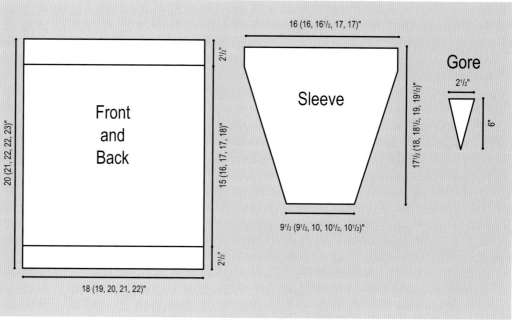

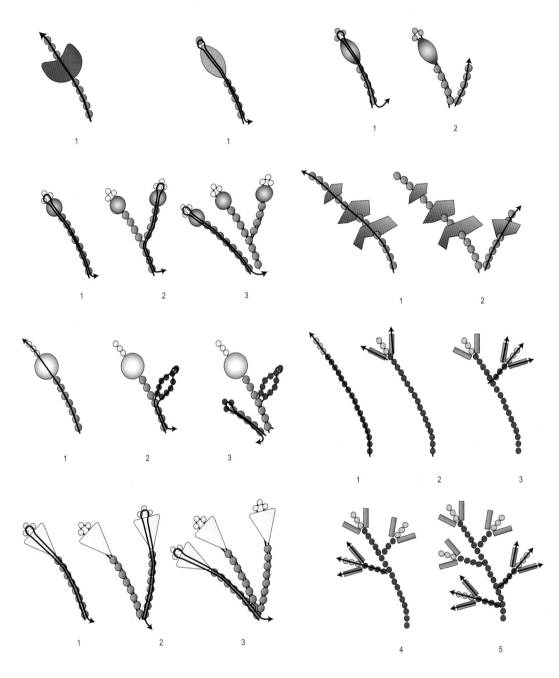

FIGURE 1

Beaded Fringe

LUMBER JILL HAT

What a change a few well-placed beads make in this easy-to-knit, rugged, red and black ribbed hat. Knit it all in black and you can accent it with any color beads you choose. The hat knits up quickly with the large needles and two strands of yarn held together as one.

SIZE

Fits 21- to 22-in (53.5 to 56 cm) head

FINISHED KNITTED MEASUREMENTS

From cuff to center top: 10½ in (26.5 cm)
Turned up cuff: 3 in (7.5 cm)
Circumference: 21 in (53.5 cm)

MATERIALS

Approx. 500 yd (450 m) of worsted-weight yarn
Approx. 35 gr of size 6 red seed beads
2 large accent beads
10 medium accent beads
Size 10½ (6.5 mm) needles, or size to obtain gauge
Size 11 beading needle
Sewing thread
Tapestry needle for sewing together seams
All purpose glue

GAUGE IN STOCKINETTE STITCH

3 sts = 1 in (2.5 cm)
4 rows = 1 in (2.5 cm)

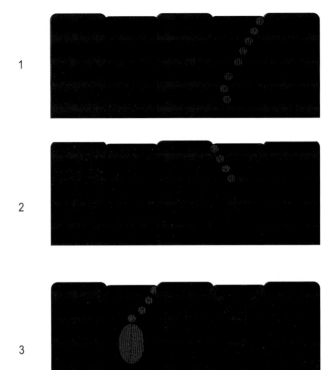

FIGURE 1

INSTRUCTIONS

Using 2 strands of yarn throughout, cast on 82 sts. Work in p2, k2 rib for 8 in (20.5 cm), ending on a wrong side row. (P2, k2tog) across next row, p2 (62 sts). P the purl sts and k the knit sts for the next two rows. (K2tog, p1) across next row, k2tog (41 sts). P the purl sts and k the knit sts for the next two rows. (P1, k1, p2tog) repeat to the last st, p1 (31 sts). K the knit sts and p the purl sts for 1 row. P1, (k1, p2tog) repeat across (21 sts). (K1, p1) repeat to the last st, p1. K2tog repeat to the last st, k1 (11 sts). Pass tail through all remaining sts twice and sew hat seam. Cut 16 pieces of yarn, each 12 in (30.5 cm) long and tie into a knot in the center. Stitch to the top of the hat.

Bead Embellishment

Thread each strand of tassel at the top of the hat and string on beads, making knots in the yarn to hold the beads at different positions on the strands. String large accent beads on 2 of the strands (make sure the knot is thick enough so the bead won't slide off). Press glue into the knots and let dry so the knots won't come out.

Using the size 10 beading needle and black thread stitch beads at the rim of the hat as shown in figure 1.

The sample project was made using 3 skeins of Encore Worsted, 75% acrylic/25% wool, 200 yd (180 m), 3.5 oz (100 gr per skein,) in color #424 Lumberjack Red by Plymouth Yarn Company.

PETITE LACE SCARF

This lacy black mohair and silk scarf is as light as air. With its touch of golden, glittering beads, it is an elegant accessory, dressy enough for eveningwear, yet understated enough for the office. Using wood or bamboo needles makes the lace work easy to control, and the five-row repeat pattern makes this an ideal weekend project for a knitter comfortable with lace knitting. Choose small or lightweight beads so that they don't weigh down the scarf too much.

FINISHED KNITTED MEASUREMENTS
4½ in (11.5 cm) wide by 45 in (114.5 cm) long

MATERIALS
1 skein of a black lace weight yarn, approximately 1 oz (25 gr), 225 yd (205 m)
Size 2 wood or bamboo knitting needles
Stitch holder
Approx. ¼ oz or 7 gr of size 11 gold-toned seed beads
10 drop beads, ⅜ in long (9.5mm)
10 beads, ¼ in long (6mm)
2 large oval beads
36 gold-toned ¼-in-long (6mm) bugle beads
22 size 8 triangle beads
Beading needle
Black beading thread

GAUGE IN STOCKINETTE STITCH
6 sts = 1 in (2.5 cm)
7 rows = 1 in (2.5 cm)

INSTRUCTIONS

Half of Scarf Beginning at Point
Cast on 4 sts. Purl all odd numbered (WS) rows.

Follow line-by-line instructions below or chart A, for right-side rows 1 through 36.

Make 9 repeats of rows 28 through 36.

Follow line-by-line instructions or chart B, rows 38 through 50, then repeat row 50 until piece measures 22 in (56 cm) when stretched slightly. Move to a stitch holder.

Line-by-line Instructions for Chart A.
Row 1 and all odd rows: (WS) purl (4 sts on first row).
Row 2: K2, yo, k2 (5 sts).

Row 4: K2, yo, k1, yo, k2 (7 sts).

Row 6: K2, yo, k2tog, yo, k1, yo, k2 (9 sts).

Row 8: K2, (yo, k2tog) twice, yo, k1, yo, k2 (11 sts).

Row 10: K2, yo, k1, yo, k2tog, k1, SKP, yo, k1, yo, k2 (13 sts).

Row 12: K2, yo, k1, yo, k2tog twice, yo, k1, SKP, yo, k1, yo, k2 (15 sts).

Row 14: K2, yo, k1, yo, k2tog, k1, k2tog, yo, k2, SKP, yo, k1, yo, k2 (17 sts).

Row 16: K2, yo, k1, yo, k2tog, k2, k2tog, yo, k3, SKP, yo, k1, yo, k2 (19 sts).

Row 18: K2, yo, k1, yo, k2tog, k2, k2tog, yo, k1, yo, SKP, k2, SKP, yo, k1, yo, k2 (21 sts).

Row 20: K2, yo, k1, yo, k2tog, k2, (k2tog, yo) twice, k1, yo, SKP, k2, SKP, yo, k1, yo, k2 (23 sts).

Row 22: K2, yo, k1, yo, k2tog, k2, (k2tog, yo, k1) twice, k1, yo, SKP, k2, SKP, yo, k1, yo, k2 (25 sts).

Row 24: K1, k2tog, yo, k4, k2tog, yo, k2, k2tog, yo, k3, yo, SKP, k4, yo, SKP, k1.

Row 26: K1, (k2tog, yo, k3) 3 times, k1, yo, SKP, k3, yo, SKP, k1.

Row 28: K1, k2tog, yo, k2, k2tog, yo, k1, yo, k2tog twice, yo, k1, yo, SKP twice, yo, k1, yo, SKP, k2, yo, SKP, k1.

Row 30: K1, (k2tog, yo, k1) twice, yo, k2tog twice, yo, k2tog, yo, k1, yo, SKP twice, yo, k1, yo, SKP, k1, yo, SKP, k1.

Row 32: K1, (k2tog, yo) twice, k1, yo, (k2tog) twice, yo, k1, k2tog, yo, k2, yo, SKP twice, yo, k1, (yo, SKP) twice, k1.

Row 34: K1, k2tog, yo, k2, yo, k2tog twice, yo, k2, k2tog, yo, k3, yo, SKP twice, yo, k2, yo, SKP, k1.

Row 36: K1, k2tog, yo, k1, yo, k2tog twice, yo, k3, k2tog, yo, k4, yo, SKP twice, yo, k1, yo, SKP, k1.

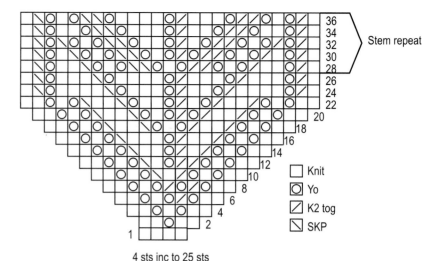

4 sts inc to 25 sts

Purl all odd number rows

	Knit
	Yo
	K2 tog
	SKP

CHART A

Line-by-line Instructions for Chart B

Row 38: K1, k2tog, yo, k2, k2tog, yo, k1, yo, k2tog twice, yo, k1, yo, SKP twice, yo, k1, yo, SKP, k2, yo, SKP, k1.

Row 40: K1, k2tog, yo, k1, k2tog, yo, k1, yo, k2tog twice, yo, k3, yo, SKP twice, yo, (k1, yo, SKP) twice, k1.

Row 42: K1, (k2tog, yo) twice, k1, yo, k2tog twice, yo, k5, yo, SKP twice, yo, k1, (yo, SKP) twice, k1.

Row 44: K1, k2tog, yo, k2, yo, k2tog, k2, SKP, yo, k3, yo, k2 tog, k2, SKP, yo, k2, yo, SKP, k1.

Row 46: K1, k2tog, yo, k1, yo, k2tog, k4, SKP, yo, k1, yo, k2tog, k4, SKP, yo, k1, yo, SKP, k1.

Row 48: K1, k2tog, yo, k8, SKP, yo, k9, yo, SKP, k1.

Row 50: K1, k2 tog, yo, k19, yo, SKP, k1.

Second Half of Scarf and Joining

Repeat directions for the first half, then graft both halves together at the center. Weave in ends.

Bead Embellishment

Thread the beading needle with a 24-in (61-cm) length of beading thread. Stitch 3 beads using a back stitch every ¼ in (6 mm) along the edge of the scarf. Sew dangles of beads onto the ends of the scarf ½ in (1.3 cm) apart, as shown in figure 1. Repeat for the other end of the scarf.

The sample project was made using 1 skein of Knit One Crochet Two, Douceur et Soie 70% baby mohair/30% silk, 1 oz (25 gr), 225 yd (205 m,) in black #542.

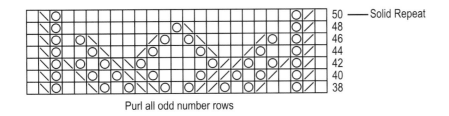

50 —— Solid Repeat
48
46
44
42
40
38

Purl all odd number rows

CHART B

FIGURE 1

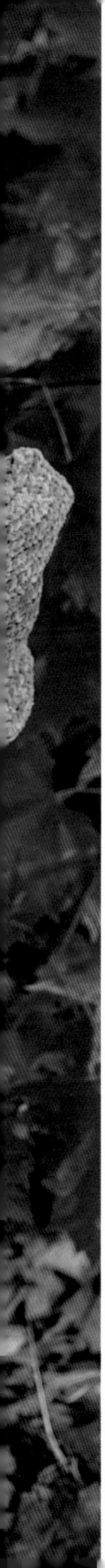

CHENILLE TUNIC

Beaded Fringe

SKILL LEVEL
INTERMEDIATE

Soft cozy chenille always works up into wonderful sweaters. In this simple design the brown clay raku beads work well with the bronze and gold tones of the other beads. They add detail and texture along the color pattern at the bottom of the tunic and sleeves.

SIZES
To fit chest sizes 34 in (36, 38, 40, 42 in), (86.5, 91.5, 96.5, 101.5, 106.5 cm). Instructions are for the smallest size, with larger sizes in parentheses. If there are no parentheses, the number is for all sizes.

FINISHED MEASUREMENTS
Bust: 40 in (42, 44, 46, 48 in), (101.5, 106.5, 111.5, 117, 122 cm).
Length: 23½ in (24, 24½, 25, 25 ½ in), (59.5, 61, 62, 63.5, 65 cm)
Upper Arm: 15 in (15 ½, 16, 16½, 17in), (38, 39.5, 40.5, 42, 43 cm)

MATERIALS
7 (7, 7, 8, 8)151 yd (140 m) skeins of worsted-weight chenille yarn
Approx. 200 yd (185 m) each of four shades of brown worsted-weight wool yarn
Size 10 (6 mm) needles, or size to obtain gauge
Stitch holders
Approx. 15 round raku beads, ⅜ in (9.5mm) diameter
Approx. ½ oz (14 gr) size 11 bronze seed beads
36 small drop beads
45 gold-toned spacer beads, ¼ in (6mm)
15 gold-toned faceted beads, ⅛ in (3mm)
15 large red-brown cylinder beads
Size 11 beading needle
Beading thread
Tapestry needle for sewing seams together.

GAUGE IN STOCKINETTE STITCH
14 sts = 4 in (10 cm)
18 rows = 4 in (10 cm)

Back

Cast on 70 (74, 78, 82, 84) sts of chenille.

Work 6 rows of seed st.

Work color border across the back, following chart A.

Continue in plain st st until piece measures 23½ in (24, 24 ½, 25, 25 ½ in), (59.5, 61, 62, 63.5, 65 cm).

Move 18 (18, 22, 22, 22) center sts to st holder. Move shoulder sts to st holder.

Front

Cast on 70 (74, 78, 82, 84) sts of chenille.

Work 6 rows of seed st.

Work color border across the front, following chart A.

Continue in plain st st until piece measures 21½ in (22, 22 ½, 23, 23 ½ in), (54.5, 56, 57, 58, 59.5 cm).

Move 16 (18, 18, 20, 22) center sts to st holder.

Working each shoulder separately, dec 1 st at neckline every other row 4 times.

Knit 4 rows even. Move rem sts to st holder.

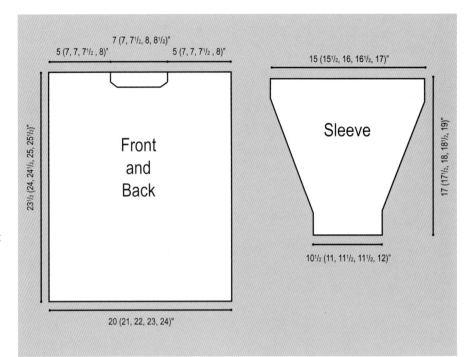

Sleeves

Cast on 37(39, 40, 40, 42) sts.

Work 4 rows of seed st.

Work color patt following chart A.

Work in st st, increasing 1 st ea side every 5 rows 8(8, 8, 9, 9) times 53 (55, 56, 56, 58) sts. Work even in st st until piece measures 18½ in (47 cm). Cast off. Repeat for other sleeve.

Assembly

Graft front and back tog at shoulder seams. Center sleeves over shoulder seam and sew in place. Sew side seams and sleeve seams.

Collar

Pick up front and back neck sts, and 6 (6, 7, 7, 7) sts on ea side of front neckline. Knit 6 rows in st st. Bind off loosely.

Bead Embroidery

Follow pattern in chart B for embroidery along color pattern on the front of the sweater and the sleeves, back stitching each strand of beads in place.

The sample project was made using 7 skeins of Rowan's Chunky Cotton Chenille, 100% cotton, 3.5 oz (100 gr), 151 yd (140 m) in parchment #383, and one skein each of Brown Sheep's Waverly Wool in four different shades of brown.

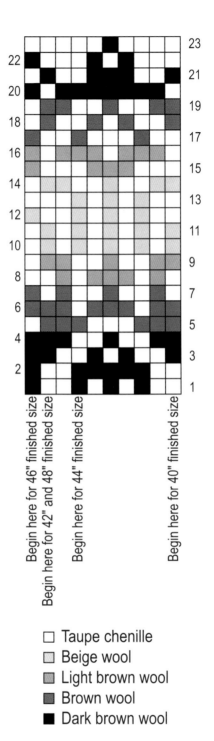

23
22
21
20
19
18
17
16
15
14
13
12
11
10
9
8
7
6
5
4
3
2
1

Begin here for 46" finished size
Begin here for 42" and 48" finished size
Begin here for 44" finished size
Begin here for 40" finished size

□ Taupe chenille
▨ Beige wool
▨ Light brown wool
▨ Brown wool
■ Dark brown wool

CHART A

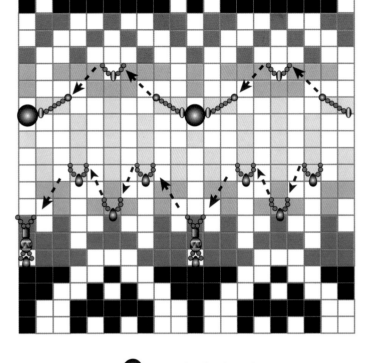

CHART B

● round raku bead
• size 11 seed bead
◓ small drop bead
◍ spacer bead
◉ faceted bead
▮ cylinder bead

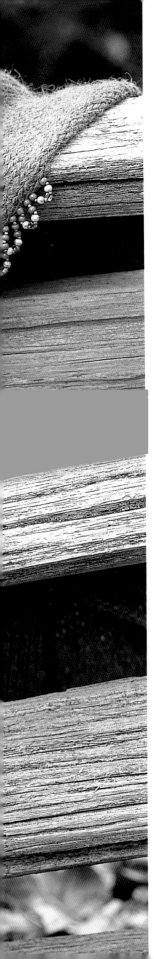

FRINGED AUTUMN SHAWL

This cozy but elegant shawl is made in simple stockinette stitch. You could substitute an allover pattern, or make it in lace for eveningwear, or in cables for a thicker wrap on cold winter nights. Also, you don't have to stitch on all the beads by hand. There are many bead fringes on the market that you could purchase and machine stitch in place if you want to make this a super-quick project.

FINISHED KNITTED MEASUREMENTS
25 in (64 cm) wide by 50 in (127 cm) long

MATERIALS
Approx. 700 yd (46 m) of sport-weight yarn
Approx. 2½ oz (70 gr) of green size 11 seed beads
Approx. ¾ oz (21 gr) of bronze size 11 seed beads
Approx. 3 oz (84 gr) of size 6 green beads
Approx. 1 oz (28 gr) of size 5 green triangle beads
Approx. 1½ oz (42 gr) of 4mm round pale green beads
Approx. ¾ oz (21 gr) of size 8 yellow seed beads
Size 7 (4.5 mm) needles, or size to obtain gauge
Size G crochet hook
Size 11 beading needle
Beading thread
Tapestry needle for sewing together seams

GAUGE IN STOCKINETTE STITCH
20 sts = 4 in (10 cm)
26 rows = 4 in (10 cm)

INSTRUCTIONS

Large Rectangle
Cast on 90 sts.

Knit in st st until the piece measures 50 in (127 cm) long.

Bind off. Weave in ends. Block.

Triangle
Cast on 80 sts.

Knit in st st, decreasing 1 st ea end every right side row until there are 2 sts left.

Bind off. Weave in ends. Block.

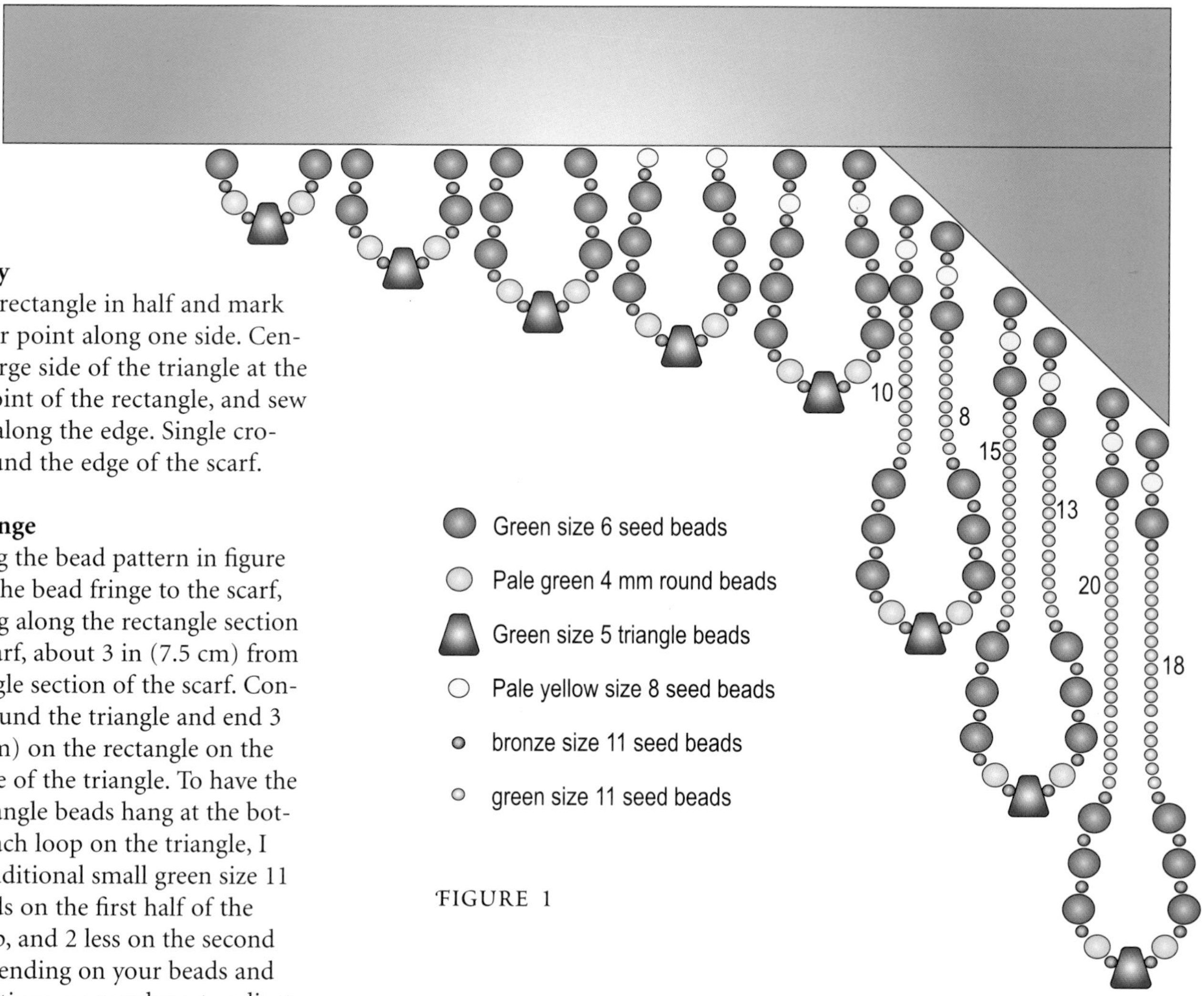

Assembly

Fold the rectangle in half and mark the center point along one side. Center the large side of the triangle at the center point of the rectangle, and sew in place along the edge. Single crochet around the edge of the scarf.

Bead Fringe

Following the bead pattern in figure 1, stitch the bead fringe to the scarf, beginning along the rectangle section of the scarf, about 3 in (7.5 cm) from the triangle section of the scarf. Continue around the triangle and end 3 in (7.5 cm) on the rectangle on the other side of the triangle. To have the size 5 triangle beads hang at the bottom of each loop on the triangle, I used 2 additional small green size 11 seed beads on the first half of the bead loop, and 2 less on the second half. Depending on your beads and your knitting you may have to adjust the difference between the number of beads so the triangle bead hangs at the bottom of the loop. When you begin the beads on the triangle, increase the number of green size 11 seed beads by 5 beads each half of the loop, until you have 40 and 38 in each strand. When you reach the point of the triangle, string 40 and 40 size 11 green seed beads in the pattern, then reverse the pattern so that you string 38 small beads first, then 40, finishing by decreasing by 5 beads, mirroring the pattern you began.

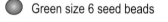

Green size 6 seed beads

Pale green 4 mm round beads

Green size 5 triangle beads

Pale yellow size 8 seed beads

bronze size 11 seed beads

green size 11 seed beads

FIGURE 1

This project was made using 6 skeins of Classic Elite's Inca Alpaca, 100% alpaca, 1.75 oz (50g), 116 yd (107 m), color #1135 Cala Cala Moss.

CARPET BAG

Rustic and sturdy, this cable-knitted bag is appliqued with bead-netted panels, using wooden beads to add another texture to the design. Adding an optional lining gives a nice finished look, and the cord closure can be decorated with beads such as the two lampworked sheep by Joan Eckard on page 57.

Beadwork
Appliqué

SKILL LEVEL
INTERMEDIATE

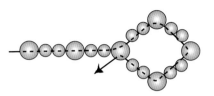

FIGURE 1

FIGURE 2

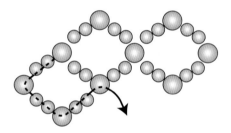

FIGURE 3

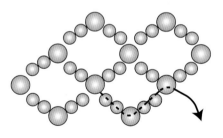

FIGURE 4

INSTRUCTIONS

Bag
Beginning at top opening, cast on 168 sts. Join into a circle, place marker.

Work in k1, p1 rib for 7 rounds.

Round 8: (K1, yo k2tog, p1) repeat around.

Continue in k1, p1 rib for 4 more rounds, then follow the cable pattern repeat in chart A 8 times around the bag. Repeat the cable pattern again, repeat the first 6 rounds once more. Work 5 rounds in reverse st st. Bind off.

Bottom of Bag
Cast on 20 sts. Knit in st st for 15 in (38 cm). Bind off.

Handles
Cast on 3 sts. Knit in seed st for 12 in (30.5 cm). Bind off. Repeat for other handle.

Beadwork
Cut a 36-in (91.5 cm) length of beading thread and thread the beading needle. String 1 small bead and tie a knot around it 6 in (15 cm) from the tail. This is a stop. It will be untied later.

Row 1 and turn around: String (1 large bead, 2 small beads) 6 times. Pass back through the fourth large bead from the needle, pull tight (figure 1).

Row 2: String 2 small beads, 1 large bead and 2 small beads. Pass through the first large bead strung, pull tight so the beads form a diamond shape (figure 2).

Turn Around: String (2 small beads, 1 large bead) twice, string 2 small beads. Pass through the large bead from row 2 (figure 3).

Row 3: String 2 small beads, 1 large bead and 2 small beads. Pass through the next large bead, pull tight so the beads form a diamond shape (figure 4).

Continue with the turn-around step then a row stitch until the netting is 10 in (25.5 cm) long. Weave in ends by passing the thread through the thread path of the beads, making a half hitch knot several times over the thread in the beads, then passing through some more beads. Cut the thread close to the beadwork. Untie the stop bead at the beginning of the beadwork and remove the stop bead, then weave in the end in the same way.

Make 4 bead netted strips.

Assembly

Sew the bottom of the bag to the body of the bag. Fold the bottom of the bag along the reverse stockinette knitted section, with the cotton cord inside, and back stitch through both layers, creating a ridge along the bottom perimeter of the bag. Repeat for the side edges of the bag.

Sew the beadwork in place along the front and back of the bag between the cables, by passing through the large beads along the edges of the beadwork, then taking a stitch in the bag. Stitch the handles in place at the top of the beadwork.

Lining (Optional)

Cut the lining fabric into an 11-by 42-in (28 x 107 cm) rectangle and a 6½-by 16-in (16.5 x 40.5 cm) rectangle. With right sides together, sew the 11-in (28 cm) sides of the large rectangle together with a ½-in (1.5-cm) seam allowance, creating a tube. Press seam open. With right-sides together, stitch one end of the tube to the perimeter of the small rectangle. Press the raw edge of the tube over ½-in (1.5 cm) to the wrong side of

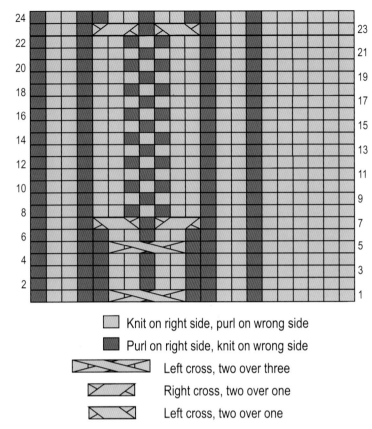

Knit on right side, purl on wrong side

Purl on right side, knit on wrong side

Left cross, two over three

Right cross, two over one

Left cross, two over one

CHART A

the fabric and place the lining inside the bag. Hand stitch in place along the top edge of the lining just below the ribbing on the knitting.

String the cording through the eyelets in the ribbing of the bag so that the cord passes twice around the bag and the ends of the cord meet at one end of the bag. Tie the cords together 3½ in (9 cm) from their ends and unravel the cord to make a tassel. Sew the decorative accent beads to the tassel.

This project was made using 2 skeins of Reynolds Lopi, 100% Icelandic wool, 3.5 oz (100 g), 110 yd (99 m), color #453 Cocoa Tweed.

PEYOTE STITCH TUNIC

Peyote stitch is one of the most popular techniques for beadworkers today. It is quick and easy compared to many other stitches, and there are countless peyote stitch pattern books available, filled with beautiful designs. There are many variations for working peyote stitch: differences in beginning and ending a row based on whether you have an odd or even number of beads; two- and three-drop stitches (using two or three beads in each stitch); even making three-dimensional pieces in sculptural peyote stitch. Any of these techniques can be adapted to knitwear, from the simple peyote stitch borders on this project to three-dimensional leaves or flowers sewn along a collar or sleeve.

SIZES

To fit chest sizes 34 in (36, 38, 40, 42 in), (86.5, 91.5, 96.5, 101.5, 106.5 cm). Instructions are for the smallest size with larger sizes in parentheses. If there are no parentheses, the number is for all sizes.

FINISHED KNITTED MEASUREMENTS

Bust: 36 in (38, 40, 42, 44 in), (91.5, 96.5, 101.5, 106.5, 111.5 cm).
Length: 25 in (25½, 26, 26, 26½ in), (63.5, 65, 66, 66, 67.5 cm).
Upper Arm: 16 in (16, 16½, 17, 17½ in), (40.5, 40.5, 42, 43, 44.5 cm).

MATERIALS

8 (9, 9, 10, 10) 126 yd (158 m) of sport-weight yarn
Approx. 3.5 oz (100 gr) of size 8 seed beads
Size 10 (5.75 mm) needles, or size to obtain gauge
Size 10 (5.75 mm) double-point needles or size to obtain gauge
Size 10 beading needle
Grey beading thread
Tapestry needle for sewing seams together

GAUGE IN STOCKINETTE STITCH HOLDING TWO STRANDS OF YARN TOG AS ONE

17 sts = 4 in (10 cm)
23 rows = 4 in (10 cm)

This tunic employs one of the simplest peyote stitch patterns. It is an excellent introduction to beadwork techniques since you will be learning a few basics while making something beautiful to add to your knitwear. The beadwork is made separately, and then stitched to the finished tunic.

The chart for peyote stitch takes some getting used to since the columns line up vertically but the rows are half a step off, like brickwork turned on its side. You stitch each row by passing through a bead of the row before, then stringing on one bead and passing through the next bead of the row before. In this way you are adding every other bead across the graph for each row. Once you get used to this pattern of "pass through a bead, pick up a bead, pass through the next bead," you will soon come to enjoy the rhythm of the technique.

INSTRUCTIONS

Note: Use 2 strands of yarn held together as 1 throughout.

Back
Cast on 3 sts.

Follow rows 1 through 17 on chart A. Break yarn leaving a 4-in (10 cm) tail to weave in later. Leave triangle on needle. Make 3 more triangles, beginning each cast-on on the empty needle so you end row 17 of the fourth triangle with all the triangles on the same needle, ready for row 18. Work row 18 of chart B, purling across all the triangles, 80 sts. For finished sizes 36 and 38 in (91.5 and 96.5 cm), work section B of chart A through row 73. For finished size, 40, 42 and 44 in (101.5, 106.5, 111.5 cm), cast on 2, 4, or 7 sts respectively, at the beginning of the next two rows, 84, 88, 94 sts. Work section C at the beginning of the row, repeat section B across the row, and work section A at the end of the row, working the number of sts indicated on the chart

for your size through row 73. (Note: For the larger sizes, this creates a straight section on the sides at the bottom edge of the tunic, between the front and back points). For finished size 36 in (91.5 cm), knit in st st in gray, decreasing 1 st ea side every fourth row, twice, 76 sts. For all sizes work even in st st in gray until back measures 25 in (25½, 26, 26, 26½ in), (63.5, 65, 66, 66, 67.5 cm). Move to st holder.

Front
Work as for the back through the colorwork pattern. Continue in st st in gray, decreasing as for back for finishes size 36 in (91.5 cm), or working even for other sides, until front measures 23 in (23½, 24, 24, 24½ in), (58, 59.5, 61, 61, 62 cm). Neckline: Move the center 22 (22, 24, 26, 26) sts to a st holder and, working ea side separately, knit in st st, decreasing 1 st on the center side every right-side row 4 times. Work even for 2 rows. Move to st holder.

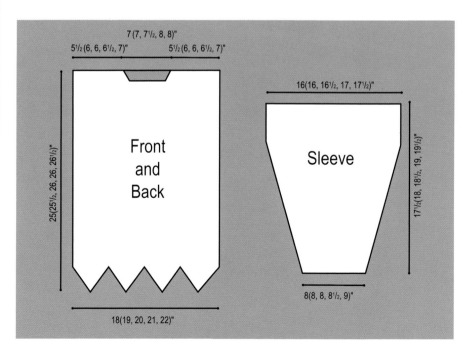

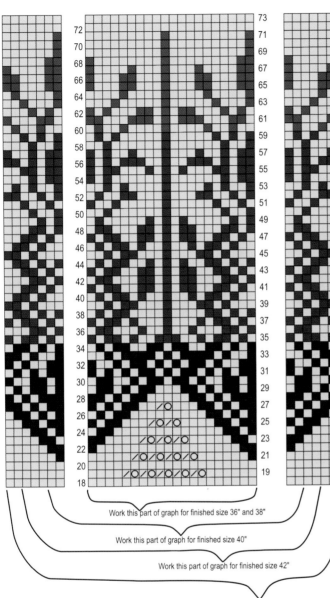

A   B   C

Work this part of graph for finished size 36" and 38"

Work this part of graph for finished size 40"

Work this part of graph for finished size 42"

Work this part of graph for finished size 44"

Sleeves

Cast on 34 (34, 34, 36, 38) sts.

Row 1: (K2tog, yo) repeat to last 2 sts, k2tog.

Knit in st st increasing 1 st ea side every fifth row, 17 (17, 18, 18, 18) times, 68 (68, 70, 72, 74) sts. Work even until sleeve measures 17½ in (18, 18½, 19, 19½ in), (44.5, 45.5, 47, 48.5, 49.5 cm). Bind off. Repeat for other sleeve.

Assembly

Graft shoulder seams tog. Center sleeve over shoulder seam. Sew sleeve to front and back. Repeat for other sleeve. Sew sleeve side seam and front and back side seam.

Neckline

Using 2 strands of gray yarn held together as 1, make 1 row of single crochet around the neckline. Weave in ends.

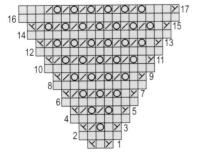

CHART A

▢ Knit on right side, purl on wrong side
⊙ Yo
⟋ K2tog
⋈ Inc 1 st
■ Two strands burgundy
■ One strand burgundy, one strand rust
■ Two strands rust
■ Two strands red
▢ Two strands gray

Beadwork

Cut a 24-in (61 cm) length of beading thread, and thread the beading needle.

Rows 1 and 2: String the 4 beads for the first 2 rows and slide them down to about 8 in (20.5 cm) from the tail of the thread. Hold the tail with your other hand so the beads won't slide off the thread and hold the beads over your index finger, as shown in figure 1.

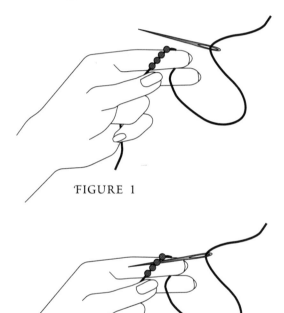

FIGURE 1

FIGURE 2

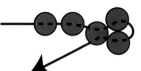

FIGURE 3

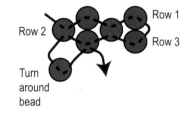

FIGURE 4

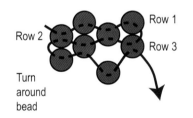

Row 2

Row 1

Row 3

Turn
around
bead

FIGURE 5

Row 2

Row 1

Row 3

Turn
around
bead

FIGURE 6

Row 3: String the first bead for row 3 and pass through the third bead away from the needle, passing the needle through the bead towards the tail end of the thread (figure 2). Hold the 3 beads between your thumb and pointer finger (while still holding the tail in your hand) and pull the thread so the beads sit as shown (figure 3). String the second bead for row 3 and pass through the last bead on the thread (closest to the tail). Pull the thread until the beads line up (figure 4).

Row 4: String 1 bead. Pass through the last bead in row 3 (figure 5). String 1 bead. Pass through the next bead in row 3 (figure 6).

Repeat row 4, stitching each row back and forth. If the beads are not staying in place as you work, hold the bead at the end of the previous row and pull the thread until the beads line up (figure 6). Continue until the beadwork is 2¾ in (7 cm) long. Make 16 beadwork strips. To attach the strips tog, use the working thread of 1 strip and pass through 2 beads on another strip (figure 7). String 1 bead and pass through the beads at the ends of the strips (figure 8). String 3 beads and pass through the beads (figure 9). Weave in the end of the thread by passing through the beads adjacent to each other and making a figure eight with the thread, locking the thread in the beadwork. Cut the thread close to the beading. Fasten 8 of the strips of beadwork tog alternating the angle, so you create a zigzag pattern.

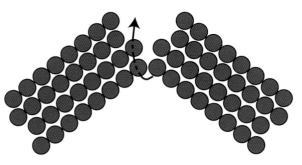

FIGURE 7

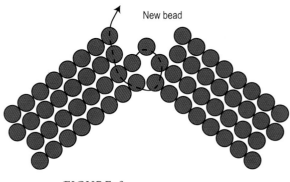

New bead

FIGURE 8

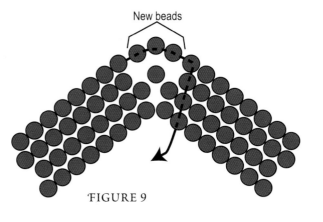

New beads

FIGURE 9

Repeat for the other 8 strips. Using the beading needle and thread, sew the finished beadwork to the bottom of the tunic just below the knitted colorwork pattern. Optional: For the larger sizes, make a strip of beadwork to fit across the side sections that don't have the points at the bottom sides of the tunic, and sew into place.

This project was made using Dale of Norway's Tiur, 60% mohair/40% wool, 1.75 oz (50 g), 126 yd (115 m), 9 skeins of #5371 dark grey, 2 skeins each of #4155 dark burgundy, #4136 rust, and # 4027 red.

BEAD-STRANDED VEST

Beadwork
Appliqué

SKILL LEVEL
CHALLENGING

🌀 *Technically, this project is not bead applique, but I put it in this section because, although you stitch the strands to the knitting while in progress, you are actually working more with the strands of beads in relation to each other rather than simply embroidering them onto the fabric.*

Working with strands of beads is a good way to cover surfaces quickly with beads. Plus, you can create some interesting effects by weaving or twisting the strands together as you stitch them in place. This bead embellishment demonstrates this technique with a small section worked on a close-fitting vest. But you could carry it further by working the pattern from top to bottom on the vest or adding more strands woven in and out of the ones already in place.

INSTRUCTIONS

Vest

Using size 6 needles, cast on 156 (160, 172, 180, 188) sts. Join into a circle, place marker. Work in k1, p1 rib for 2½ in (6.5 cm).

Change to size 8 needles. Knit in st st until tube is 11½ in (12, 12½, 12½, 12½), (29, 30.5, 32, 32, 32 cm), at each side, bind off 8 sts evenly divided from front and back. Place front sts on st holder.

Back

Continue in st st decreasing 1 st ea side every row 4 times for armholes. Decrease 1 st at ea side every other row 7 times, 48 (50, 56, 60, 64) sts. Work even until back measures 16½ in (17½, 18½, 18½, 19½ in), (42, 44.5, 47, 47, 49.5 cm). Move center 22 (22, 24, 26, 30) sts to st holder. Working ea shoulder separately, work 1 row in st st, on the next row, move 2 more sts on each shoulder to st holder 11

SIZES

To fit chest sizes 34 in (36, 38, 40, 42 in), (86. 5, 91.5, 96.5, 101.5, 106.5 cm). Instructions are for the smallest size, with larger sizes in parentheses. If there are no parentheses, the number is for all sizes.

FINISHED KNITTED MEASUREMENTS

Bust: 36 in (38, 40, 42, 44 in), (91.5, 96.5, 101.5, 106.5, 111.5 cm)
Length: 18 in (19, 20, 20, 21 in), (45.5, 48, 51, 51, 53.5 cm)

MATERIALS

3 (3, 3, 3, 4) 172yd (115 m) skeins of worsted-weight yarn
Approx. 1 oz (28 g) of size 11 seed beads
18 size 5 triangle beads
72 size 8 seed beads
Size 8 (5 mm) 29-in (74-cm) circular needle, or size to obtain gauge
Size 6 (4 mm) 29-in (74-cm) circular needle
Size 11 beading needle
Stitch holders
Beading thread
Tapestry needle for sewing together seams

GAUGE IN STOCKINETTE STITCH

17 sts = 4 in (10 cm)
23 rows = 4 in (10 cm)

(12, 14, 15, 15) shoulder sts, 26 (26, 28, 30, 34) sts on stitch holder. Work ea shoulder even until vest measures 18 in (19, 20, 20, 21 in), (45.5, 48.5, 51, 51, 53.5 cm). Move shoulder sts to st holders.

Front

Pick up front sts from st holder. Work the armholes the same as for the back. At the same time, after working 2 rows, working ea side separately, dec 1 st at center front every knit row 13 (13, 14, 15, 17) times. Work even until front measures 18 in (19, 20, 20, 21 in), (45.5, 48.5, 51, 51, 53.5 cm).

Graft front to back at shoulder seams.

Neckline and Armholes

Pick up 72 (76, 80, 84, 88) sts along armhole and knit in k1, p1 rib for 6 rounds. Bind off loosely. Repeat for the other armhole.

Pick up 86 (90, 96, 100, 106) sts along neckline, including 26 (26, 30, 34) sts from stitch holder, and knit in k1, p1 rib for 6 rounds, making a centered double dec at center front every round. Bind off loosely.

Beadwork

Step 1: Beginning 8 sts to the right of center front, 1 row below the point of the ribbing of the neckline, string 1 size 8 seed bead, then enough size 11 seed beads to drape to the center front stitch, then 1 more size 8 seed bead. (Using figure 1, refer to 1.) Pass through the center front stitch, then string 1 size 8 bead, 1 size 5 triangle and 1 size 8 seed bead, and pass through the center stitch again (refer to 2). String 1 size 8 seed bead, then the same number of size 11 seed beads as before, then 1 more size 8

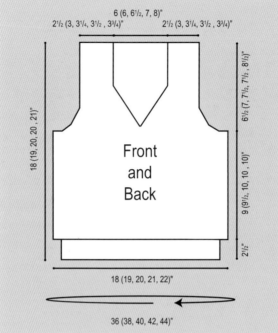

seed bead and stitch through the eighth stitch on the left of center front, coming out of the stitch 4 rows below (refer to 3). Make the same pattern of beads below the first, back in the opposite direction, ending with the thread coming four rows below the last strand of beads (refer to 4, 5, and 6). Repeat the pattern twice more. Pass the needle up to 1 stitch below the end of the first repeat on the right side.

Stringing the same number of beads in each step above, pass over and under the strands of beads from the pattern in figure 1, following the pattern and steps in figure 2. Repeat until all the strands are twisted.

Make another column of strands of beads stitched between the overlap of the previous strands. Add 2 small strands at the top of the design (figure 3).

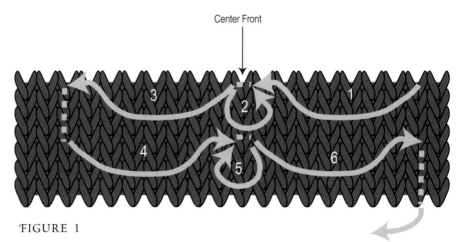

FIGURE 1

Center Front

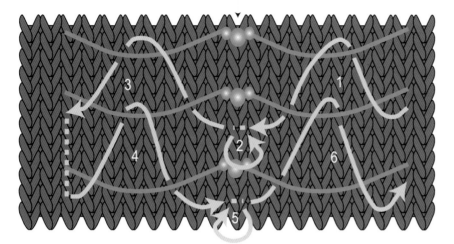

FIGURE 2

Center Front

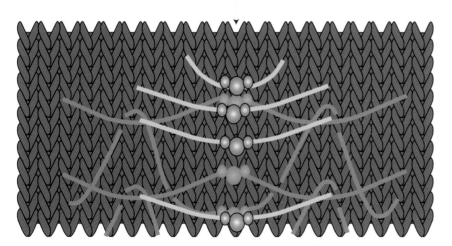

FIGURE 3

This project was made using 3 skeins of Reynolds Harmony, 100% wool, 4 oz (112 g), 172 yd (158 m), color #3 plum.

BEADS ON THE YARN

The following three sections—Beads Over Slip Stitch, Beaded Knitting, and Bead Knitting—cover techniques that are most purely knitting with beads. Beads are strung onto the yarn and then slid in front of, between, or onto the stitches as they are made. The beads can be sprinkled across the surface, or slid into each stitch to form a color pattern or shape. One color of beads can be strung onto the yarn, or you can follow a color chart, carefully stringing a pattern to be knit into the fabric.

BEADS OVER SLIP STITCH

In this technique, before beginning to knit, string beads onto the yarn you will be using. When working on the knit side, when you reach the stitch where the pattern shows a bead, bring the yarn to the front of your work, slide a bead down to the

needle, slip the next stitch purlwise from the left needle to the right needle, then bring the yarn to the back of the work, and continue knitting. When working on the purl side, when you reach a stitch where the pattern shows a bead, bring the yarn to the back of the work (the knit side on this row), slide a bead down to the needle, slip the next stitch purlwise from the left needle to the right needle, then bring the yarn to the front of the work (the purl side of this row) and continue purling. This causes the bead to hang on a horizontal strand of yarn in front of the slipped stitch. You can also slide several beads in front of one slipped stitch to make a small loop of beads, or slide several beads in front of two or three slipped stitches in a row to make a horizontal stripe of beads. But with this stitch, you can't make a vertical line of beads since you would be slipping the same stitch again and again, and the garment would never get knitted. However, you can do it

every other row, still affording a lot of possibilities, depending on the size of beads you use and your pattern.

BEADED KNITTING

Hard to believe, but bead knitting and beaded knitting are not the same. In bead knitting you slide a bead into the stitches you knit. The beads are all on the front of the finished knitting, sitting on one strand of a specific stitch. In beaded knitting you slide one or more beads between stitches, traditionally in garter stitch, so that the beads hang at the back of the current row. Because every row of garter stitch is a knit row, you end up with beads on the front and the back of the finished knitting.

Beaded knitting is the technique used for swag purses popular in the 1920s. These bags were distinguished by vertical bands of beads tapering to points at the top of the bag. It is the easiest technique for working with pre-strung beads in knitting. Beads are strung onto the yarn before beginning, and then one or more beads are slid between stitches. To do this you simply knit to the place where the bead is indicated in the pattern, then slide a bead up to the needle and continue knitting. The bead will sit on the front of the knitting if you purl both stitches next to the bead and on the back of the knit-

ting if you knit both stitches. You can slide one or more beads between stitches. The more beads, the wider the knitting will be at that point. As you do this, the strand of beads will hang in a graceful arc from the weight of the beads. Most antique purses were knit in garter stitch so there was a double thickness of beads throughout the purse since each row was a knit row allowing the beads to hang at the back of the current row. The Denim Tank Top, Denim Purse, and Cascading Diamonds Scarf are made using a variation of this technique.

BEAD KNITTING

Bead knitting is the process of pre-stringing beads onto the yarn before knitting, then pushing the beads, one at a time, into each stitch indicated on the pattern. (If you are using different colors of beads, you string them in reverse color sequence.) With this process, you can fill the whole surface (as in the knitted purses of the late 1800s and early 1900s), or you can use one color of beads, forming a pattern on the knitted fabric, which is a variation of plaited stockinette stitch.

On the charts for bead knitting using the plaited stockinette stitch variation, you may notice that some of the designs look as if the beads are in the wrong place, just a little off from where they should be. This is because the graph is in straight columns and rows, but when you create plaited knitting, the stitches (and therefore the beads) slant to the right in the knit row, and to the left in the purl row. So, when you knit your project you will see the beads fall into place as in the sample projects, rather than looking a little off as in the charts. If, when you are knitting you find that your beads are way off from where they should be, double check; you may be knitting the purl rows, and purling the knit rows!

ABOUT BEADS ON THE YARN

For these projects you will need a variety of different needles, including variously sized knitting needles, tapestry needles for sewing knitted seams, and beading needles to stitch beads together. Beading needles are longer and thinner than most sewing needles and come in sizes that loosely correspond to bead sizes, from size 10 to size 16. The trick is to find the largest needle possible, so it is easier to thread, but which will still fit through the smallest beads you are using for your project. (A size 16 needle is much smaller than a size 10. A size 10 needle will go through most size 11 beads and is the easiest to thread.)

When stringing beads onto yarn for pre-strung projects, you have several options. You can use a needle that has a large enough eye to thread the yarn, yet is thin enough to pass through the beads. If this is not possible, you can tie a thread over the yarn, so the yarn is folded in half, and thread a beading needle with the thread. This way you can string beads with smaller holes, carefully sliding them onto the folded yarn. Or you can use specialty needles. One such variety has points at both ends and a large collapsing opening in the middle, making it easy to thread the yarn and string beads (the points at both ends can be a hazard though). Another specialty needle is a wire needle with a collapsible eye. These are made from wire folded in half and twisted, and come in different thickness. In the supply lists for the

instructions I have indicated "needle to string the beads onto the yarn," rather than listing a specific needle, since which you choose will depend on your preference.

Working with beads strung onto the knitting yarn is a simple idea, but there are some basic techniques that make working with the beads and yarn easier.

Beads can be embroidered or sewn to a garment made of almost any kind of yarn, but there are limitations to the types of yarn that can be used for pre-strung projects with beads since the yarn must fit through the bead hole. The bead can slide loosely on the yarn, or fit snugly. Some yarns can be damaged by the friction of beads sliding along them, so it is wise to test a small piece of yarn by running the beads you want to use along it several times to see how well it stands up. Acceptable yarn will be relatively regular in diameter (no thick and thin hand-spun effects, no nubby boucle). It is difficult, but not impossible, to knit with beads on multiple strands of yarn since one strand will often lag behind, especially if the yarns vary in thickness or type. The easiest yarn to work with when knitting with beads is soft, resilient, and uniform. Beads will easily slide into place and stay where you want them. This type of yarn is also somewhat forgiving if your tension is a bit too tight or too loose.

After you have all your beads on the yarn, you need to be able to have enough bare yarn available to knit your project, yet still have enough beads close to your working area on the yarn to slide easily into the knitting as you work. Leave the number of beads needed for the first row up

near the beginning of the yarn, and slide the rest of the beads about 4 feet (1 m) away. You will then need to move beads up for each row, and slide the rest of the beads further down the yarn.

To slide beads along yarn, always slide a small amount at a time, usually not more than 3 to 4 in (7 to 10 cm) of beads, so that the action of sliding the beads on the yarn abrades the yarn as little as possible. For these projects, I have placed all the beads for a specific section onto the yarn at once. Some yarns are more easily worn down by the action of sliding beads along them; if you need to substitute yarn, be sure to slide some beads along it first to see if it will hold up to the abrasion.

Since you are pulling out long amounts of yarn from your skein which are now covered with beads, you need to have a way to keep your yarn from getting into a tangled mess as you work. Many knitters wrap the bead-covered yarn back around the skein to keep it corralled. I don't like this technique since you are constantly unwrapping it again to move beads either toward your knitting to knit them into the piece, or away from your work so you have bare yarn to knit. I always place my skein of yarn in a basket and slide the beads down the yarn so the yarn and beads pile loosely there. This way all the elements are together so I can move them easily to wherever I want to work, the yarn doesn't get tangled, and I don't ever have to wind and unwind yarn to move beads.

Checking your gauge is extremely important when knitting a garment with an intended size, but less important when making something,

such as a scarf, which can vary in width and length. When knitting with beads, there are times when gauge is crucial. Gauge is important in bead knitting where the goal of the technique is to fill each stitch with a bead color to create the intended design. If your gauge is too loose, the beads won't sit next to each other and the design will look scattered and sketchy, and you may have most of your beads sliding around to the back of the work. If your gauge is too tight, your stitches will change in size from where the beads are to where there are no beads in the knitting. (This is not an issue if all the stitches are filled with beads, such as in antique bead knitted purses). The gauge is determined by a combination of your tension, the thickness of the yarn and knitting needles, and the size of the beads. It's important to make test swatches to get the proper tension and gauge so beads appropriately fill the space of the stitch. The same is true for stranding beads in front of your knitting (Beads Over Slip Stitch) where you want the bead or beads to fill the strand of yarn in front of the slipped stitch. In beaded knitting the gauge isn't as important to the bead part of the project, though it is still just as important to achieve the proper gauge for garment sizing, and to make your stitches tight enough on either side of the bead or beads so there isn't a gap of yarn.

CHECKERED HAT

This basic stockinette stitch hat with a rolled edge is a great project for trying this technique. Here you slide a bead in front of every other stitch along the row. Try it in simple black and white, as shown, or in bold colors, changing beads and yarn colors with each row.

INSTRUCTIONS

Beginning at the Bottom Rim
Cast on 116 sts.

Knit in st st for 3½ in (9 cm). Break yarn, string the beads onto the yarn and tie to the working strand.

On the next row (k1, bring the yarn forward, slide a bead down to the needle, slip the next st purlwise, bring the yarn to the back) repeat to the last 2 sts, k2.

Purl the next row.

On the next row k1 (k1, bring the yarn forward, slide a bead down to the needle, slip the next st purlwise, bring the yarn to the back) repeat to the last st, k1.

Purl the next row.

Repeat the last 4 rows.

Knit in st st for 4 in (10 cm).

Decreases for top of hat, beginning on a right side row:

Row 1: (K7, k2tog) repeat to the last 8 sts, k8 (104 sts).
Row 2, and all even rows: Purl.
Row 3: (K6, k2tog) repeat across (91 sts).
Row 5: (K5, k2tog) repeat across (78 sts).
Row 7: (K4, k2tog) repeat across (65 sts).
Row 9: (K3, k2tog) repeat across (52 sts).

Row 11: (K2, k2tog) repeat across (39 sts).
Row 13: (K1, k2tog) repeat across (26 sts).
Row 15: k2tog repeat across (13 sts).

Cut the yarn to about 24 in (61 cm) and thread a tapestry needle; then pass through the remaining sts and stitch the side seam tog. Roll up the rim of the hat (it will do this on its own) to just below the beadwork and stitch in place. Mist with warm water, shape if necessary, and let dry in a warm place.

SIZES
To fit 22-in (56 cm) head circumference

FINISHED KNITTED MEASUREMENTS
From bottom (after stitching the rolled cuff in place) to center top: 9 in (23 cm)
Circumference: 22 in (56 cm)

MATERIALS
Approx. 250 yd (230 m) of dk-weight yarn
228 matte black size 5 triangle beads large enough to string onto the yarn
Size 7 (4.5 mm) needles or size to obtain gauge
Needle to thread beads onto yarn
Tapestry needle for sewing together seams

GAUGE IN STOCKINETTE STITCH
20 sts = 4 in (10 cm)
24 rows = 4 in (10 cm)

The sample project was made using one 8-ply wool pak of Baabajoes yarn 100% wool 525 yd (485 m), 70 oz (250 gr) per skein, color #1, natural.

LACY BLOUSE

Beads Over Slip Stitch

SKILL LEVEL
CHALLENGING

This is the perfect project if you want to try a little knitting with beads, but don't want to use beads throughout. The small inset of beaded knitting works up quickly and the blouse design is simple rectangles with just a small amount of decreasing on the sleeves. Make the short blouse, as shown, or keep knitting and create an over-sized long tunic or dress.

SIZES
To fit chest sizes 34 in (36, 38, 40, 42 in), (86.5, 91.5, 96.5, 101.5, 106.5 cm). Instructions are for the smallest size, with larger sizes in parentheses. If there are no parentheses, the number is for all sizes.

FINISHED KNITTED MEASUREMENTS
Bust: 36 in (38, 40, 42, 44 in), (91.5, 96.5, 101.5, 106.5, 111.5 cm)
Length: 18½ in (19, 20, 21, 21 in), (47, 48.5, 51, 53.5, 53.5 cm)
Upper Arm: 17 in (17½, 18, 18½, 19 in), (43, 44.5, 45.5, 47, 48.5 cm)

MATERIALS
11 (11, 12, 12, 13) 93 yd (85 m) skeins of sport-weight yarn
Approx. 1 oz (28 gr) of size 6 beads that can fit on the yarn
Size 6 (4 mm) needles, or size to obtain gauge
Needle to string the beads onto the yarn
Tapestry needle for sewing together seams

GAUGE IN STOCKINETTE STITCH
20 sts = 4 in (10 cm)
28 rows = 4 in (10 cm)

INSTRUCTIONS

Back
Cast on 90 (96, 100, 106, 110) sts. Work in st st for 4 rows. Work the next row (k1, yo, k2tog) repeat across. Continue in st st until back measures 10 in (10½, 11, 11½, 11½ in), (25.5, 26.5, 28, 29, 29 cm) from row 5. Cast off 32 (35, 37, 40, 42) sts at the beg of the next 2 rows. Continue knitting for 6½ in (7, 7, 7½, 7½ in), (16.5, 18, 18, 19, 19 cm) Bind off.

Front
Cast on 90 (96, 99, 105, 111) sts. Work in st st for 4 rows. Work the next row (k1, yo, k2tog) repeat across. Continue in st st for 7 rows.

Follow chart A, repeating until front measures 10 in (10½, 11, 11½, 11½ in), (25.5, 26.5, 28, 29, 29 cm) from row 5. Bind off.

Inset with Beads

String the beads onto the yarn. Cast on 25 sts. Follow pattern in chart B. Bind off.

Sleeves

Cast on 45 (45, 48, 51, 54) sts. Work in st st for 4 rows. Work the next row in (k1, yo, k2tog) repeat across. Continue in st st, increasing 1 st ea side, every knit row, 20 (21, 21, 21, 21) times. Work even until piece measures 14½ in (15, 15½, 16, 16½ in), (37, 38, 39, 40.5, 42 cm). Bind off.

Assembly

Block all pieces to diagram dimensions, adding ¾ in (2 cm) to the length of the sleeves and front and back for turning under the hem at row 5. On every piece except the inset, fold the bottom edge to the inside at row 5 (the yo row) and stitch hem in place, creating a small scalloped edge. Press flat. Center inset at top of front and stitch in place. Stitch shoulder portion of sleeves to front, inset sides, and back. Stitch seams of sleeves and front and back side seams tog. Weave in ends.

This project was made using 2 skeins of Classic Elite's Imagine Space Dyed 53% cotton/47% rayon, 1.75 oz (50 g), 930 yd (850 m).

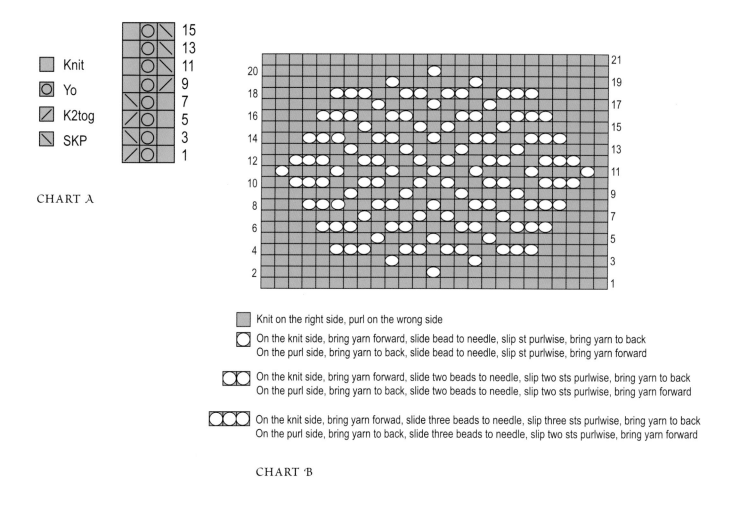

CHART A

- □ Knit
- ◯ Yo
- ⊘ K2tog
- ◺ SKP

Knit on the right side, purl on the wrong side

On the knit side, bring yarn forward, slide bead to needle, slip st purlwise, bring yarn to back
On the purl side, bring yarn to back, slide bead to needle, slip st purlwise, bring yarn forward

On the knit side, bring yarn forward, slide two beads to needle, slip two sts purlwise, bring yarn to back
On the purl side, bring yarn to back, slide two beads to needle, slip two sts purlwise, bring yarn forward

On the knit side, bring yarn forwad, slide three beads to needle, slip three sts purlwise, bring yarn to back
On the purl side, bring yarn to back, slide three beads to needle, slip two sts purlwise, bring yarn forward

CHART B

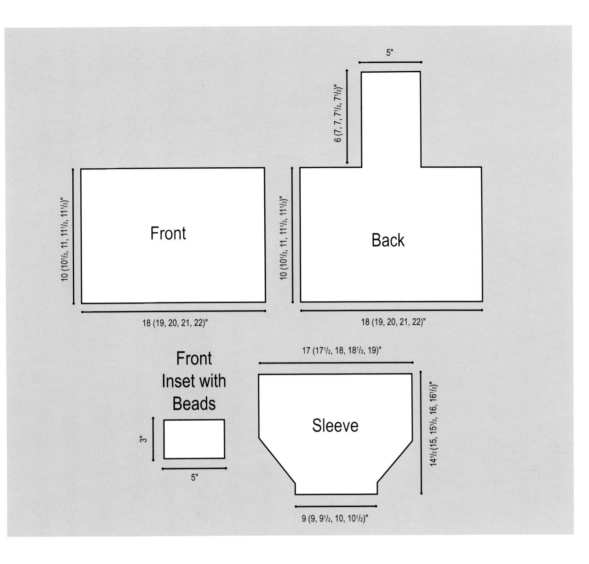

Front

10 (10½, 11, 11½, 11½)"

18 (19, 20, 21, 22)"

5"

6 (7, 7, 7½, 7½)"

Back

10 (10½, 11, 11½, 11½)"

18 (19, 20, 21, 22)"

Front
Inset with
Beads

3"

5"

17 (17½, 18, 18½, 19)"

Sleeve

14½ (15, 15½, 16, 16½)"

9 (9, 9½, 10, 10½)"

SHAWL-COLLAR TUNIC

🌀 *This design takes advantage of yarn that is available in
both bulky and worsted weights. It knits up quickly in
the bulky yarn, yet allows you to add beading detail with the same
yarn in the worsted-weight center panel. If you can't find the same
yarn in the two weights, you can use a contrasting color for the
center panel, or try two strands of yarn in place of the bulky
weight, and one strand for the worsted-weight section.*

SIZES

To fit chest sizes 34 in (36, 38, 40, 42 in), (86.5, 91.5, 96.5, 101.5, 106.5 cm).
Instructions are for the smallest size, with larger sizes in parentheses. If there
are no parentheses, the number is for all sizes.

FINISHED KNITTED MEASUREMENTS

Bust: 36 in (38, 40, 42, 44 in), (91.5, 96.5, 101.5, 106.5, 111.5 cm)
Length: 24 in (24, 25, 25, 25½ in), (61, 61, 63.5, 63.5, 65 cm)
Upper Arm: 17 in (17, 18, 18, 18½ in), (43, 43, 45.5, 45.5, 47 cm)

MATERIALS

7 (8, 8, 9, 9) 143 yd (132 m) skeins of bulky-weight yarn
One 200 yd (185 m) skein of worsted weight yarn
192 size 6 seed beads
Size 10 (5.75 mm) needles, or size to obtain gauge
Size 8 (5 mm) needles
Needle to string beads onto the yarn
Tapestry needle for sewing together seams

GAUGE IN STOCKINETTE STITCH USING SIZE 10 NEEDLES

15 sts = 4 in (10 cm)
17 rows = 4 in (10 cm)

INSTRUCTIONS

Back

Using the size 10 needles and the bulky-weight yarn, cast on 68 (72, 75, 79, 82) sts. Work in moss st for 6 rows. On the next row k the purl sts and p the knit sts. Work in st st until the piece measures 21 in (21, 22, 22, 22½ in), (53.5, 53.5, 56, 56, 57 cm). On the next row (k1, p1) repeat across. Work in moss st beginning by knitting the purl sts and purling the knit sts of the previous row. Continue in moss st until the piece measures 24 in (24, 25, 25, 25 1/2 in), (61, 61, 63.5, 63.5, 65 cm). Bind off.

FRONT SIDE PANELS
Right side

Using the size 10 needles and the bulky weight yarn, cast on 24 (26, 28, 30, 32) sts. Work in moss st for 6 rows. On the next row k the purl sts and p the knit sts. Work in st st until the piece measures 16 in (40.5 cm). To begin the neckline, continue in st st, decreasing 1 st at center side every fourth row 7 times, 17 (19, 21, 23, 25) sts. Work 1 row of (k1, p1) repeat across. Work even in moss st, beginning by knitting the purl sts and purling the knit sts of the previous row. Continue in moss st until the piece measures 24 in (24, 25, 25, 25½ in), (61, 61, 63.5, 63.5, 65 cm). Bind off.

Left side

Work as for the right side, decreasing for the neckline on the opposite side of the knitting.

CENTER BEAD PANEL

Slide the beads onto the worsted-weight yarn. Using the size 8 (5 mm) needles, cast on 25 sts. Work in moss st for 8 rows. On the next row k the

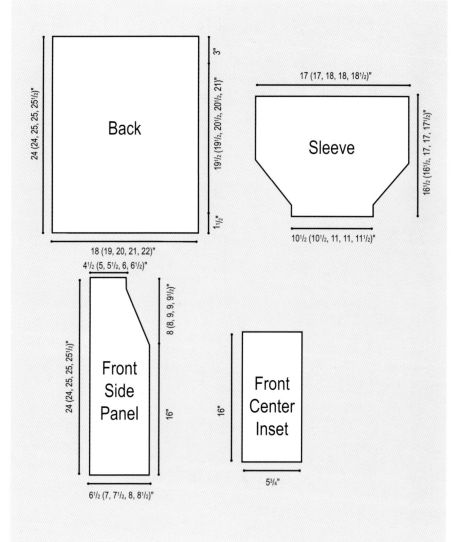

purl sts and p the knit sts. Continue in st st for 3 rows. Follow chart A repeating these 30 rows. Bind off.

Sleeves

Using the size 10 (5.75 mm) needles and the bulky-weight yarn, cast on 39 (39, 41, 41, 44) sts. Work in moss st for 6 rows. On the next row knit the purl sts and purl the knit sts. Work in st st, increasing 1 st ea side every fourth row, 13 times, 65 (65, 67, 67, 70) sts . Work even until sleeve measures 16½ in (16½, 17, 17, 17½ in), (42, 42, 43, 43, 44.5 cm). Bind off. Repeat for the other sleeve.

Assembly

Stitch the front side panels to the center bead panel. Stitch the front and back shoulder seams together. Center the sleeves over the shoulder seam and stitch in place. Sew the sleeve seams and front to back side seams.

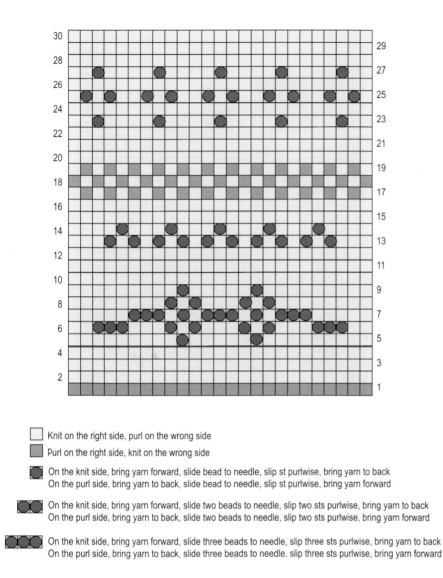

Knit on the right side, purl on the wrong side

Purl on the right side, knit on the wrong side

On the knit side, bring yarn forward, slide bead to needle, slip st purlwise, bring yarn to back
On the purl side, bring yarn to back, slide bead to needle, slip st purlwise, bring yarn forward

On the knit side, bring yarn forward, slide two beads to needle, slip two sts purlwise, bring yarn to back
On the purl side, bring yarn to back, slide two beads to needle, slip two sts purlwise, bring yarn forward

On the knit side, bring yarn forward, slide three beads to needle, slip three sts purlwise, bring yarn to back
On the purl side, bring yarn to back, slide three beads to needle. slip three sts purlwise, bring yarn forward

CHART A

Collar

Using the size 10 (5.75 mm) needles and the bulky weight yarn, pick up 32 (32, 35, 35, 37) sts along one front side, 26 (26, 28, 28, 29) along the back neckline, and 32 (32, 35, 35, 37) along the other front side. Knit in k1, p1 rib for 6 in. Bind off loosely.

Stitch the ends of the collar to the top center bead panel. Weave in ends.

This project was made using Plymouth's Encore, 75% acrylic/25% wool, 3.5 oz (100 g), 8 skeins bulky, 143 yd (132 m), 1 skein worsted 200 yd (185 m), color #240, light beige.

CASCADING DIAMONDS SCARF

Here I have used large iridescent beads in a sampling based on an old purse pattern that would have been used as an allover pattern for a bag worked in silk thread and small seed beads. The use of specific increases, by knitting into the back of the strand between stitches, gives a clean-finished look to the bead pattern at the scarf ends. To help you visualize the finished beadwork, I have included a bead pattern below the knitting chart.

FINISHED KNITTED MEASUREMENTS
9½ in (24 cm) wide x 60 in (153.5 cm) long

MATERIALS
Approx. 425 yd (392 m) of worsted-weight yarn
1,450 size 5 seed beads with holes large enough to string onto the yarn
Size 8 (5 mm) needles, or size to obtain gauge
Needle to thread beads onto yarn
Tapestry needle for grafting together seams

GAUGE IN STOCKINETTE STITCH
18 sts = 4 in (10 cm)
23 rows = 4 in (10 cm)

INSTRUCTIONS
String half of the beads onto ea skein of yarn (725 beads on ea skein).

Follow the line-by-line instructions below, or the pattern in chart A through row 26. Repeat row 26 until scarf is 30 in (76 cm), (half the desired length). Repeat for the other skein of yarn. Graft the two pieces tog. Weave in ends.

Line-by-line Instructions
Using a simple cast on, (cast on 2 sts, slide 8 beads) repeat 8 times, cast on 2 sts.

Row 1: K1, (p1, B7, p1) repeat 8 times, k1.
Row 2: P1, (k1, B6, k1) repeat 8 times, p1.
Row 3: K1, p1, (B5, p1, B1, p1) repeat 7 times, B5, p1, k1.

Row 4: P1, k1, (B4, k1, B2, k1) repeat 7 times, B4, k1, p1.

Row 5: K1, p1, (B3, p1, B3, p1) repeat 7 times, B3, p1, k1.

Row 6: P1, k1, (B2, k1, B4, k1) repeat 7 times, B2, k1, p1.

Row 7: K1, p1, (B1, p1, B5, p1) repeat 7 times, B1, p1, k1.

Row 8: P2, k1, B6, k1, B1, k1, B6, k2, B6, k1, B1, k1, B6, k1, B1, k1, B6, k2, B6, k1, B1, k1, B6, k1, p2.

Row 9: K2, M1a, p1, B5, p1, B1, p1, B5, p1, M1a, p1, B5, p1, B1, p1, B5, p1, B1, p1, B5, p1, M1b, p1, B5, p1, B1, p1, B5, p1, M1b, k2.

Row 10: P3, k1, B4, k1, B2, k1, B4, k1, p1, k1, B4, k1, B2, k1, B4, k1, B2, k1, B4, k1, p1, k1, B4, k1, B2 k1, B4, k1, p3.

Row 11: K3, M1a, p1, B3, p1, B3, p1, B3, p1, k1, M1a, p1, B3, p1, B3, p1, B3, p1, B3, p1, B3, p1, M1b, k1, p1, B3, p1, B3, p1, B3, p1, M1b, k3.

Row 12: P4, k1, B2, k1, B4, k1, B2, k1, p2, k1, B2, k1, B4, k1, B2, k1, B4, k1, B2, k1, p2, k1, B2, k1, B4 k1, B2, k1, p4.

Row 13: K4, M1a, p1, B1, p1, B5, p1, B1, p1, k2, M1a, p1, B1, p1, B5, p1, B1, p1, B5, p1, B1, p1, M1b, k2, p1, B1, p1, B5, p1, B1, p1, M1b, k4.

Row 14: P6, k1, B6, k1, p5, k1, B6, k1, B1, k1, B6, k1, p5, k1, B6, k1, p6.

Row 15: K6, M1a, p1, B5, p1, k5, M1a, p1, B5, p1, B1, p1, B5, p1, M1b, k5, p1, B5, p1, M1b, k6.

Row 16: P7, k1, B4, k1, p6, k1, B4, k1, B2, k1, B4, k1, p6, k1, B4, k1, p7.

Row 17: K7, M1a, p1, B3, p1, k6, M1a, p1, B3, p1, B3, p1, B3, p1, M1b, k6, p1, B3, p1, M1b, k7.

Row 18: P8, k1, B2, k1, p7, k1, B2, k1, B4, k1, B2, k1, p7, k1, B2, k1, p8.

Row 19: K8, p1, B1, p1, k7, M1a, p1, B1, p1, B5, p1, B1, p1, M1b, k7, p1, B1, p1, k8.

Row 20: P19, k1, B6, k1, p19.

Row 21: K19, M1a, p1, B5, p1, M1b, k19.

Row 22: P20, k1, B4, k1, p20.

Row 23: K20, M1a, p1, B3, p1, M1b, k20.

Row 24: P21, k1, B2, k1, p21.

Row 25: K21, p1, B1, p1, k21.

Row 26: Purl

Row 27: Knit

Repeat row 26 and 27 until the piece measures 30 in (76 cm). Repeat for the other skein of yarn. Graft the two pieces tog. Weave in ends.

This project was made using 2 skeins of Knit One, Crochet Too's Parfait Solids 100% wool, 3.5 oz (100 g), 218 yd (201 m), color #1730 eggplant.

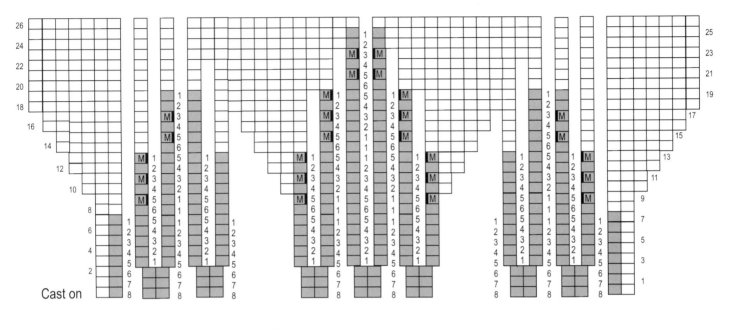

Cast on

□ Knit on the right side, purl on the wrong side

▨ Purl on the right side, knit on the wrong side

Ⓜ Make one stitch by knitting into the back of the strand after the current stitch

Ⓜ Make one stitch by knitting into the back of the strand before the current stitch

1 Slide the number of beads indicated between stitches

CHART A

Bead pattern

DRESSED-UP SWEATER

The addition of beads to a plain, simple sweater design such as this one makes a casual piece of clothing just a little bit dressy. The details on the sleeves add sophistication to the design.

SIZES
To fit chest sizes 34 in (36, 38, 40, 42 in), (86.5, 91.5, 96.5, 101.5, 106.5 cm). Instructions are for the smallest size, with larger sizes in parentheses. If there are no parentheses, the number is for all sizes.

FINISHED KNITTED MEASUREMENTS
Bust: 36 in (38, 40, 42, 44 in), (91.5, 96.5, 101.5, 106.5, 111.5 cm)
Length: 22 in (23, 24, 24½, 25 in), (56, 58, 61, 62, 63.5 cm)
Upper Arm: 15 in (15½, 16, 16½, 17 in), (38, 39.5, 40.5, 42, 43 cm)

MATERIALS
8 (9, 9, 10, 11) 1.75 oz (50 gr) skeins 103 yd (95 m) of a dk-weight yarn
Approx. 30 gr of size 6 cream seed beads
Size 7 (4.5 mm) needles, or size to obtain gauge
Size 7 (4.5 mm) 20-in (51 cm] circular needles for collar
Stitch holders
Size 10 beading needle
Sewing thread
Tapestry needle for sewing seams together

GAUGE IN STOCKINETTE STITCH
5 sts = 1 in (2.5 cm)
6 rows = 1 in (2.5 cm)

INSTRUCTIONS

Back
Cast on 90 (96, 100, 106, 110) sts. K2, p2 rib for 3 ¾ in (4, 4½, 4½, 4 ¾ in), (9.5, 10, 11.5, 11.5, 12 cm). Work in st st until piece measures 10 in (10½, 11, 11, 11½ in), (25.5, 26.5, 28, 28, 29 cm).

Armhole Shaping
Bind off 5 sts at beg of next 2 rows. Dec 1 st ea side every other row 3 (4, 5, 6, 7) times 74 (78, 80, 84, 86) sts. Work even until armhole measures 8 in (8½, 8½, 9, 9 in), (20, 21.5, 21.5, 23, 23 cm).

Shoulder and Neck Shaping

Bind off 7 sts at beg of next 4 (4, 4, 0, 0) rows, 8 sts at beg of next 2 (2, 2, 6, 4) rows, 9 sts at beg of next 0 (0, 0, 0, 2) rows. Place rem 30 (34, 36, 36, 36) sts on holder.

Front

Work same as back to Armhole Shaping. Decrease for armholes same as back, and then break off the working yarn and string 316 (330, 338, 358, 366) beads onto a new skein of yarn. Attach to the current row and knit the bead pattern in chart A for each right side row, knitting the first and last 2 stitches in st st and beginning the first repeat at the specified column, then repeating the pattern across the row, from right to left, and completing a partial repeat of the pattern at the end of each row. Purl all wrong side rows.

When the bead pattern is completed, continue even in st st until armholes measure 7, 7½, 7½, 8, 8 in (18, 19, 19, 20.5, 20.5 cm).

Shoulder and Neck Shaping

Place 8 (14, 16, 16, 16) center sts on holder. Working the sides simultaneously, place 0 (1, 1, 1, 1) st at ea side of center onto the st holder for the next 4 rows. Begin Shoulder Shaping as for back while continuing to place one center st on holder on ea right side row.

Sleeves

String 45 beads onto a new skein. Beginning at cuff, cast on 36 (38, 40, 42, 44) sts.

Row 1: K2 (3, 4, 5, 6), (k2, p1, B1, p2, B1, p1) 5 times, k4 (5, 6, 7, 8)

Row 2 and all wrong-side rows: P.

Row 3: K1 (2, 3, 4, 5), (k4, p1, B1, p1) 5 times, k5 (6, 7, 8, 9).

Continue in st st, following bead pattern in chart B, while increasing 1 st ea side, every fourth row, beginning with the seventh row, until there are 78 (80, 82, 82, 84) sts. Work even in st st until piece measures 15¾ in (16, 16, 16, 16½ in) (40, 40.5, 40.5, 40.5, 42 cm).

Cap Shaping

Bind off 6 sts at beg of next 2 rows. Dec 1 st ea side every other row 15 (15, 16, 16, 17) times, 36 (38, 38, 38, 38) sts. Dec 1 st ea side every row 6 times 24 (26, 26, 26, 26) sts, Bind off 8 sts at the beg of the next 2 rows, bind off remaining 8 (10, 10, 10, 10) sts.

Finishing

Block all pieces to measurements. Sew front to back at shoulders and side seams. Move all stitches at neckline to 20-in (51-cm) circular needles and knit in k2, p2 rib for 6 in (15 cm). Turn to wrong side and bind off loosely, beginning at center back. Weave in ends. Sew sleeve seams. Sew sleeves in arm holes.

This project was made using 7 (8, 8, 9, 9) skeins of Bluefaced Leicester, 100% pure new wool, 1.75 oz (50 g), 103 yd (95 m), color #7009 deerskin by Berroco.

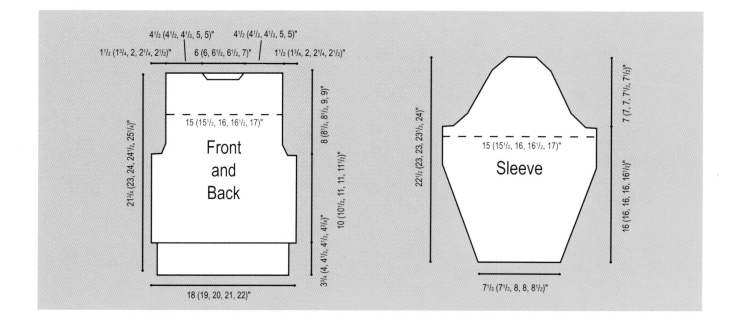

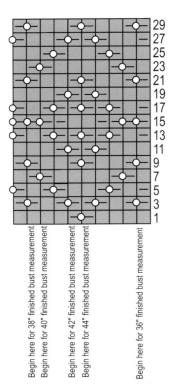

Begin here for 38" finished bust measurement
Begin here for 40" finished bust measurement
Begin here for 42" finished bust measurement
Begin here for 44" finished bust measurement
Begin here for 36" finished bust measurement

29
27
25
23
21
19
17
15
13
11
9
7
5
3
1

 Knit on right side, purl on wrong side
Purl on right side, knit on wrong side
Slide a bead between stitches

Purl all even numbered rows

CHART A

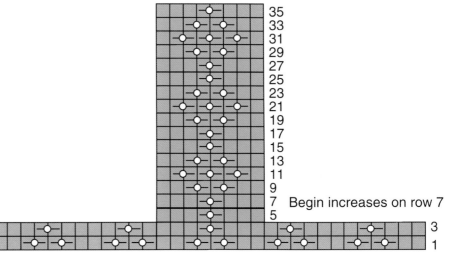

35
33
31
29
27
25
23
21
19
17
15
13
11
9
7   Begin increases on row 7
5
3
1

Purl all even numbered rows

CHART B

Beaded Knitting

SKILL LEVEL
CHALLENGING

Dressed-Up Gloves

With only a touch of beadwork, transform a practical accessory into an elegant addition to any winter wardrobe. These gloves, with tapered fingers and a thumb gusset, are enhanced by both the beads and the cable pattern. When made with the same yarn, they match the Dressed-Up Sweater to create an ensemble.

SIZE
To fit medium women's hand, approximately 4 in (10 cm) across palm.

FINISHED KNITTED MEASUREMENTS
Cuff length: 5 in (12/5 cm)
Total length: 12½ in (32 cm)

MATERIALS
Approx. 200 yd worsted-weight yarn
24 size 6 cream seed beads
Size 4 (3.5 mm) 8-in (20.5-cm) double-pointed needles, or size to obtain gauge
Size 10 beading needle
Sewing thread
Tapestry needle
Stitch markers

GAUGE IN STOCKINETTE STITCH
6 sts = 1 in (2.5 cm)
7 rows = 1 in (2.5 cm)

INSTRUCTIONS

LEFT GLOVE

Cuff and Body

Slide 12 beads onto the yarn and cast on 44 sts. Join into a circle, placing a marker at the beginning of the round. (This marks the right side "seam" of the glove as indicated on chart A). Work in k2, p2 rib for 5 in. For the next 5 rows, knit the first 6 sts in the round in st st, continue the rib pattern over the next 14 of the center back sts, and work the remaining sts in st st. These are rows 1 through 5 on chart A. On the sixth row beg the thumb gusset by increasing 1 st on either side of the st 10 sts to the right of the rib pattern on the center back of the glove. Continue working the body, following chart A, moving the gusset sts onto a contrasting strand of yarn and casting on 8 new sts to make thumb hole, on row 19. Continue in st st and cable pattern for 14 more rows. Move all sts to a contrasting yarn.

Thumb

Pick up the sts along the thumb hole and 2 sts on each side, 21 sts total. Knit 2 rounds, then decrease 1 st at each side of thumb, 19 sts. Continue in st st, decreasing 2 sts after 4 rounds, then again after 4 more rounds, 15 sts total. Knit 4 more rounds. Distribute sts so there are 5 sts on each of 3 needles. Make 3 evenly spaced double decreases, 9 sts. Knit 1 round. Make 3 more double decreases above previous decreases. Cut yarn and weave through last 3 sts, weave in end.

Index Finger

Beg as indicated on chart A, picking up 14 sts for the index finger, and cast on 2 more sts for the gap between fingers, 16 sts. Knit in the round in st st, decreasing 1 st at each side on the eighth and sixteenth rounds, 12 sts total. Knit 4 more rounds. On the fifth round (make a double decrease, then K1) 3 times. On the seventh round, k2tog 3 times. Cut yarn and weave through last 3 sts, weave in end.

Middle Finger

For the middle finger, pick up 2 sts from the side of the index finger, 6 sts from the back of the hand, cast on 2 more sts between the back and the palm, and 6 sts from the palm, 16 sts. Work the same as for the index finger, except decrease on the tenth and eighteenth rounds, then finish the same.

Ring Finger

Pick up 2 sts from the middle finger, 7 sts from the back of the hand, cast on 1 more st for the gap between fingers and pick up 6 sts from the palm, 16 sts. Work the same as for the index finger.

Little Finger

Pick up the remaining 13 sts and 1 st from the ring finger, 14 sts. Work as for the index finger, except decrease on the fourth and ninth rounds, 10 sts, then knit 2 more rounds and k2tog around for the next 2 rounds, then cut the yarn and weave through the last sts, weaving in the end.

Finishing

Weave in any loose ends. Block glove to smooth decreases.

RIGHT GLOVE

Make the same as for the left glove, reversing the finger and thumb placements.

This project was made using 2 skeins of Bluefaced Leicester, 100% pure new wool, 1.75 oz (50 g), 103 yd (95 m), color #7009 deerskin by Berroco.

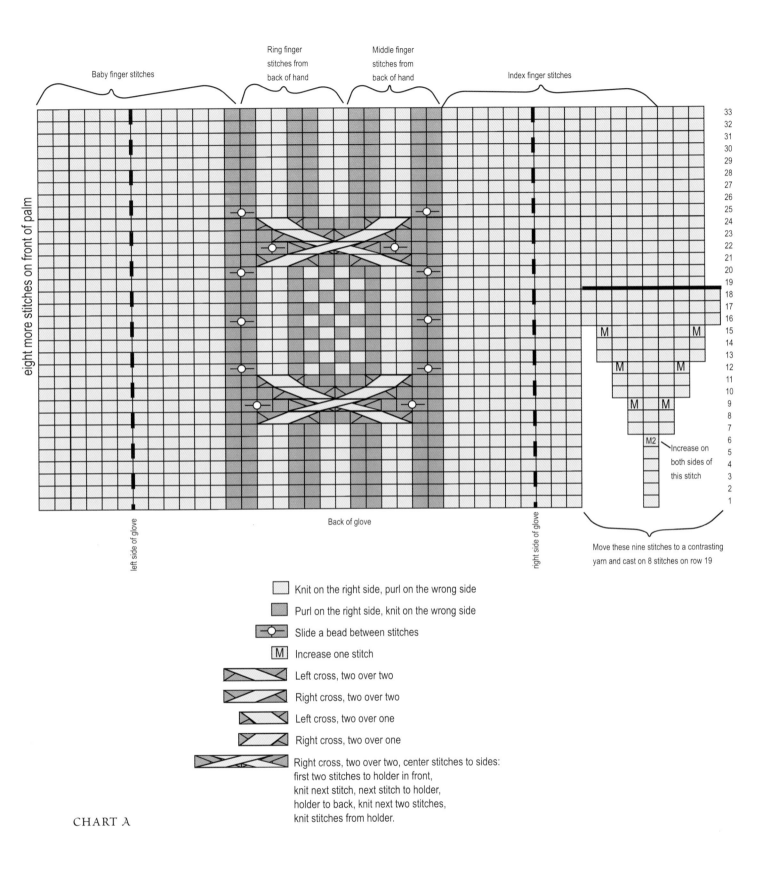

Baby finger stitches

Ring finger
stitches from
back of hand

Middle finger
stitches from
back of hand

Index finger stitches

eight more stitches on front of palm

left side of glove

Back of glove

right side of glove

Move these nine stitches to a contrasting
yarn and cast on 8 stitches on row 19

Increase on
both sides of
this stitch

Knit on the right side, purl on the wrong side

Purl on the right side, knit on the wrong side

Slide a bead between stitches

M — Increase one stitch

Left cross, two over two

Right cross, two over two

Left cross, two over one

Right cross, two over one

Right cross, two over two, center stitches to sides:
first two stitches to holder in front,
knit next stitch, next stitch to holder,
holder to back, knit next two stitches,
knit stitches from holder.

CHART A

DENIM TANK TOP

⟲ *This little tank top is a perfect demonstration of the casual side of bead knitting. The bead gores go through the washer and dryer with the denim knitting and come out ready for a leisurely stroll on the beach. The side zipper and fitted waist make this a flattering design.*

SIZES
To fit chest sizes 34 in (36, 38, 40, 42 in), (86.5, 91.5, 96.5, 101.5, 106.5 cm). Instructions are for the smallest size, with larger sizes in parentheses. If there are no parentheses, the number is for all sizes.

FINISHED KNITTED MEASUREMENTS
Bust: 35 in (37, 39, 41, 43 in), (89, 94, 99, 104, 109 cm)
Length: 18 in (20, 21, 22, 22 in), (46, 51, 53.5, 56, 56 cm)

MATERIALS
8 (8, 9, 9, 9,10) 93 yd (85 m) skeins of worsted-weight denim yarn
1428 (1564, 1700, 1768, 1904) size 6 seed beads with holes large enough to string onto the yarn
Size 6 (4 mm) 32-in-long (81-cm) circular needles, or size to obtain gauge
Stitch holders
Stitch markers
Needle to string beads onto yarn
Tapestry needle for sewing together seams
7 in (9, 9, 9, 9 in), (18, 23, 23, 23, 23 cm) zipper

GAUGE IN STOCKINETTE STITCH BEFORE WASHING
19 sts = 4 in (10 cm)
24 rows = 4 in (10 cm)

INSTRUCTIONS

Body
String 1428 (1564, 1700, 1768, 1904) beads onto one ball of yarn.

Keeping 140 beads on the tail side of the yarn, make a slip knot on the needle about 3 yd (2.5 m) from the tail end of the yarn. Slide all but 140 of the beads on the skein side of the yarn down to the skein so there are about 3 yd of yarn without beads.

Cast on 130 (140, 150, 162, 170) sts, sliding 5 beads on each yarn end after the first 5 (4, 3, 6, 4) sts and then after every 6 sts, then cast on the last 5 (4, 3, 6, 4) sts, 21 (23, 25, 26, 28) bead sections, 130 (140, 150, 162, 170 sts total).

Beginning on the Right Side
Row 1: K5 (4, 3, 6, 4), B5 (k6, B5) repeat 20 (22, 24, 25, 27) times, k5 (4, 3, 6, 4).
Row 2: P4 (3, 2, 5, 3), k1, B5, k1 (p4, k1, B5, k1) repeat 20 (22, 24, 25, 27) times, p4 (3, 2, 5, 3).
Rows 3 and 4: Repeat row 1 and row 2.
Row 5: K5 (4, 3, 6, 4), B4, (k6, B4) repeat 20 (22, 24, 25, 27) times, k5 (4, 3, 6, 4).
Row 6: P4 (3, 2, 5, 3), k1, B4, k1 (p4, k1, B4, k1) repeat 20 (22, 24, 25, 27) times, p4 (3, 2, 5, 3).
Rows 7 and 8: Repeat row 5 and row 6.
Row 9: K5 (4, 3, 6, 4), B3, (k6, B3) repeat 20 (22, 24, 25, 27) times, k5 (4, 3, 6, 4).
Row 10: P4 (3, 2, 5, 3), k1, B3, k1 (p4, k1, B3, k1) repeat 20 (22, 24, 25, 27) times, p4 (3, 2, 5, 3).
Rows 11 and 12: Repeat row 9 and row 10.
Row 13: K5 (4, 3, 6, 4), B2, (k6, B2) repeat 20 (22, 24, 25, 27) times, k5 (4, 3, 6, 4).
Row 14: P4 (3, 2, 5, 3), k1, B2, k1 (p4, k1, B2, k1) repeat 20 (22, 24, 25, 27) times, p4 (3, 2, 5, 3).
Rows 15 and 16: Repeat row 13 and row 14.
Row 17: K5 (4, 3, 6, 4), B1, (k6, B1) repeat 20 (22, 24, 25, 27) times, k5 (4, 3, 6, 4).
Row 18: P4 (3, 2, 5, 3), k1, B1, k1 (p4, k1, B1, k1) repeat 10 (11, 12, 12, 13) times, place marker (left side seam), (p4, k1, B1, k1) repeat 10 (11, 12, 13, 14) times, p4 (3, 2, 5, 3).

Work in st st, increasing 4 sts every fourth row, 9 times, making the increases 2 sts from ea end and 2 sts from both sides of the marker, 166 (176, 186, 196, 206) sts total.

Work even until piece measures 11 in (12, 12½, 13, 13 in), (28, 30.5, 32, 33, 33 cm), in total length. Move front half of knitting to stitch holder, remove marker, 83 (88, 93, 98, 103) sts each side.

Back Shaping
Working in st st, bind off 5 sts at ea side seam, 73 (78, 83, 88, 93) sts.

Dec 1 st ea side every row 4 (5, 6, 6, 7) times, 65 (68, 71, 76, 79) sts.

Dec 1 st ea side every other row 5 (6, 6, 7, 8) times, 55 (56, 59, 62, 63) sts.

Work even for 5 more rows.

Bind off 11 (12, 15, 18, 19) center sts, 22 sts remaining each side.

Working ea side separately, dec 1 st at center side every row 4 times.

Dec 1 st at center side every other row 6 times (12 sts total).

Work even until armhole measures 11 in (12, 12½, 13, 13 in), (28, 30.5, 32, 33, 33 cm).

Place stitches on stitch holder.

Front Shaping
Working in st st, bind off 5 sts at ea side seam, 73 (78, 83, 88, 93) sts.

Dec 1 st ea side every row 4 (5, 6, 6, 7) times, 65 (68, 71, 76, 79) sts.

Dec 1 st ea side every other row 5 (6, 6, 7, 8) times, 55 (56, 59, 62, 63) sts.

At the same time, on the fifth dec row, bind off 11 (12, 15, 18, 19) center sts and, working ea side separately, dec 1 st at center on next 4 rows, then every other row, 6 times (12 sts total).

Work even until armhole measures 11 in (12, 12½, 13, 13 in). (28, 30.5, 32, 33, 33 cm).

Finishing
Graft front and back shoulders tog. Stitch top 2 in (1, 1½, 2, 2 in), (5,.2.5, 4, 5, 5 cm) of left side seam tog. Make a single row of backward crochet along the armhole and neck edges.

(Backward crochet is a nice finish for knitted and crocheted garments. It is a relatively new technique in which you work single crochet stitches towards the right, rather than the left. This creates large bumps or bobbles along the edge of the garment. You need to make the stitches very loose to keep the same tension as the finished knitting. To do this, attach the yarn at the center back of the neckline edge. Insert the hook from the right side to the wrong side, into the edge of the neckline about ¼ in (6 mm) to the right of where the yarn is attached. Wrap the yarn around the hook, then pull the hook through the edge of the neckline, so you end up with 2 loops remaining on the hook. Wrap the yarn around the hook and pull through the 2 remaining loops. You have just made a single crochet, working to the right, instead of the left. Make the stitch loosely and you will create a large bobble with each stitch. Continue working around to the right.)

Weave in ends. Machine-wash and dry following the yarn manufacturer's instructions to shrink length by 20 percent. Steam iron any curling edges flat. Machine-stitch zipper at side seam with zipper opening at bottom edge.

The sample project was made using 9 skeins of Rowan Yarn's Denim, 100% cotton, 85 yd (93 m), 1.75 oz (50 gr) per skein, color #225 Nashville.

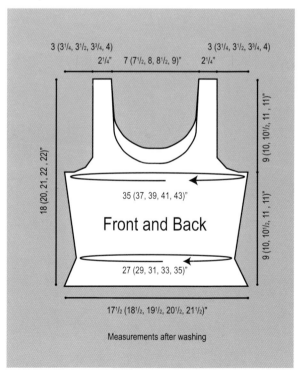

3 (3¼, 3½, 3¾, 4)
2¼" 7 (7½, 8, 8½, 9)"
3 (3¼, 3½, 3¾, 4)
2¼"

9 (10, 10½, 11, 11)"

9 (10, 10½, 11, 11)"

18 (20, 21, 22, 22)"

35 (37, 39, 41, 43)"

Front and Back

27 (29, 31, 33, 35)"

17½ (18½, 19½, 20½, 21½)"

Measurements after washing

DENIM BAG

Here is the perfect accessory to the Denim Tank Top or, on its own, a casual purse for any day you wear blue jeans. The lining and beads give the bag personality. The sample project has an ocean feel, but you could line the bag with a red bandana and use white beads for a sporty look, or use shiny black beads and satin for something chic.

INSTRUCTIONS

Body

String 476 beads onto yarn.

Cast on 50 sts, keeping 35 beads on tail side of yarn and sliding 5 beads up to the needle on each yarn after the first 7 sts, and then after every 6 sts, 6 times, then cast on the last 7 sts.

Beginning on the Right Side

Row 1: K7, B5 (k6, B5) repeat 6 times, k7.
Row 2: P6, k1, B5, k1 (p4, k1, B5, k1) repeat 6 times, p6.
Rows 3 and 4: repeat row 1 and row 2.
Row 5: K7, B4, (k6, B4) repeat 6 times, k7.
Row 6: P6, k1, B4, k1 (p4, k1, B4, k1) repeat 6 times, p6.
Rows 7 and 8: Repeat row 5 and row 6.
Row 9: K7, B3, (k6, B3) repeat 6 times, k7.
Row 10: P6, k1, B3, k1 (p4, k1, B3, k1) repeat 6 times, p6.

Rows 11 and 12: Repeat row 9 and row 10.
Row 13: K7, B2, (k6, B2) repeat 6 times, k7.
Row 14: P6, k1, B2, k1 (p4, k1, B2, k1) repeat 6 times, p6.
Rows 15 and 16: Repeat row 13 and row 14.
Row 17: K7, B1, (k6, B1) repeat 6 times, p7.
Row 18: P6, k1, B1, k1 (p4, k1, B1, k1) repeat 5 times, p6.

Work 15 more rows in st st then cast on 66 sts and join into a circle. Knit in the round in st st until bag is 17 in (43 cm) from first cast on. Mark side seams (4 sts from sides of flap) and make centered double decrease at each side seam every other row 3 times.

Graft front and back together. Weave in ends.

Purse Strap

Cast on 12 sts and knit a flat strip in st st 28 in (71 cm) long. Weave in ends. Roll long edges into center of strip as if you were rolling up a scroll. The smooth side of the strap should be 8 sts wide. Where the curled edges on the other side meet, stitch together using beading or sewing thread and a sewing needle, adding a bead between each st. Sew strap ends securely ½ in (1.5 cm) inside bag just beyond each side of flap.

Machine wash and dry the finished bag following the yarn manufacturer's instructions. Steam iron any curling edges flat.

Lining (Optional)

Fold the fabric in half and place the finished bag with the flap closed over the fabric, lining up the folded edge of the fabric with the bottom of the bag. Cut the fabric ¼ in (6 mm) larger than the bag all around. With right sides together, stitch the side seams with a ¼-in (6-mm) seam allowance. Do not turn right side out. Press seams open. Fold over the top edge of the lining ¼ in (6 mm) to the wrong side (outside) of the lining. Fit the lining in the bag, pin to the edge of the bag and hand sew in place.

The sample project was made using 3 skeins of Rowan Denim, 100% cotton, 85 yd (93 m), 1.75 oz (50 gr) per skein, color #225 Nashville.

AUTUMN–LEAVES BERET

Bead
Knitting

SKILL LEVEL
CHALLENGING

Making the small triangle pieces of this detailed hat helps break the project into manageable sections. You can also alter the design by only bead knitting every other section or changing colors of yarn and/or beads for each section, giving the hat your distinctive creative stamp.

INSTRUCTIONS

Triangle Section

String all the beads for 1 section onto the brown yarn, following the design chart A, stringing from right to left, then from left to right, as indicated by the arrows.

Cast on 41 sts, using two of the size 1 needles, making a false row to pick up later for ribbing. Follow the pattern in chart A or the line by line instructions below to knit 1 triangle section. Working in twisted stockinette stitch throughout, add 1 bead in each stitch as indicated, leaving the rest of the stitiches without beads.

Rows 1-3: (0) Knit.
Row 4: (0) Knit in twisted stockinette st.
Row 5: (5) P12, B2, p19, B3, p5.
Row 6: (9) K5, B4, k18, B3, k2, B2, k7.
Row 7: (10) P3, B1, p3, B3, p1, B3, p2, B2, p14, B1, p8.
Row 8: (12) K8, B2, k13, B3, k1, B3, k1, B3, k3, B1, k3.
Row 9: (18) P4, B6, p1, B3, p1, B4, p8, B3, p1, B2, p8.
Row 10: (23) SKP, k5, B8, k4, B2, k2, B3, k1, B10, k2, k2tog (39 sts total).
Row 11: (24) P5, B8, p1, B3, p1, B4, p3, B9, p5.
Row 12: (24) SKP, k3, B3, k1, B6, k3, B4, k1, B11, k3, k2tog (37 sts total).
Row 13: (24) P5, B16, p2, B3, p1, B2, p1, B3, p4.
Row 14: (23) SKP, k2, B3, k1, B3, k1, B2, k3, B15, k3, k2tog (35 sts total).
Row 15: (19) P4, B4, p1, B8, p5, B1, p2, B3, p1, B3, p3.
Row 16: (20) SKP, k1, B3, k1, B4, k6, B9, k1, B4, k2, k2tog (33 sts total).
Row 17: (20) P4, B3, p1, B10, p5, B5, p1, B2, p2.
Row 18: (17) SKP, k1, B1, k2, B5, k4, B7, k1, B2, k2, B2, k2, k2tog (31 sts total).

Row 19: (16) p7, B6, p1, B4, p3, B5, p2, B1, p2.
Row 20: (14) SKP, k3, B5, k3, B4, k1, B3, k1, B2, k5, k2tog (29 sts total).
Row 21: (13) P7, B1, p1, B3, p1, B4, p3, B5, p4.
Row 22: (10) SKP, k3, B4, k3, B4, k2, B2, k7, k2tog (27 sts total).
Row 23: (7) P13, B3, p3, B4, p4.
Row 24: (2) SKP, k4, B2, k17, k2tog (25 sts total).
Row 25: (1) P18, B1, p6.
Row 26: (0) SKP, k21, k2tog (23 sts total).
Row 27: (2) P12, B2, p9.
Row 28: (3) SKP, k8, B3, k8, k2tog (21 sts total).
Row 29: (3) P9, B3, p9.
Row 30: (3) SKP, k8, B3, k6, k2tog (19 sts total).
Row 31: (4) P7, B4, p8.
Row 32: (4) SKP, k7, B4, k4, k2tog (17 sts total).

Row 33: (4) P6, B4, p7.
Row 34: (5) SKP, k5, B5, k3, k2tog (15 sts total).
Row 35: (4) P5, B4, P6.
Row 36: (4) SKP, k4, B4, k3, k2tog (13 sts total).
Row 37: (3) P5, B3, p5.
Row 38: (3) SKP, k3, B3, k3, k2tog (11 sts total).
Row 39: (1) P6, B1, p4.
Row 40: (1) SKP, k2, B1, k4, k2tog (9 sts total).
Row 41: (1) P5, B1, p3.
Row 42: (1) SKP, k2, B1, k2, k2tog (7 sts total).
Row 43: (1) P3, B1, p3.
Row 44: (0) SKP, k3, k2tog (5 sts total).
Row 45: (0) P5.
Row 46: (0) SKP, k1, k2tog (3 sts total).
Row 47: (0) P3.
Row 48: (0) K3tog (1 st total).

Weave in end or leave end 6 in (15 cm) long to use for bead dangles at center top of hat.

Make 5 more triangles.

Assembly, Ribbing, and Finishing
Stitch triangles together into a circle. Using size 1 (2.25 mm) double-pointed needles, pick up the false row of stitches at the base of the triangles all around the circle (246 sts). Mark the beginning of the round.

Work in moss stitch for the first 8 rounds as follows:

Rounds 1, 2, 5, and 6: (k1, p1) repeat around.

Rounds 3, 4, 7, and 8: (p1, k1) repeat around.

Change to the size 3 (3.25 mm) needles and holding 2 strands of yarn together as 1 throughout, knit in k2, p2 rib for 1½ inches (4 cm). Bind off loosely. Weave in ends. Block to shape, drying over a plate to form the beret shape. String beads to the center top of the hat to make acorns and leaves as shown in figure 1.

The sample project was made using 2 1.75 oz (50 gr) 215 yd (197 m) skeins of Wildfoote Luxury Sock Yarn, 75% washable wool/25% nylon, color #12 bark cloth by Brown Sheep.

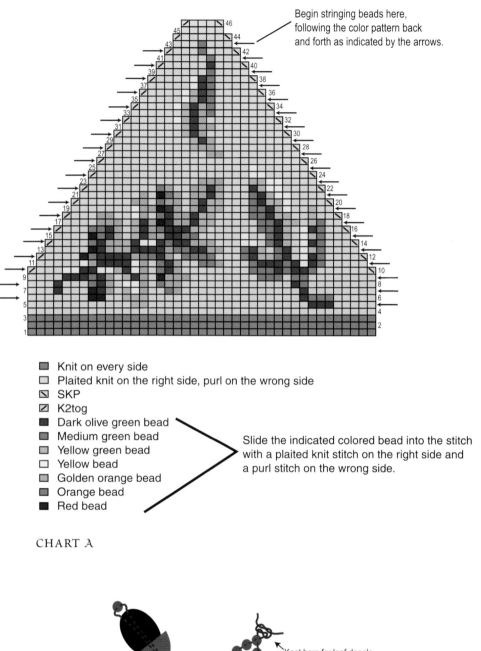

Begin stringing beads here, following the color pattern back and forth as indicated by the arrows.

- ■ Knit on every side
- □ Plaited knit on the right side, purl on the wrong side
- ◨ SKP
- ◪ K2tog
- ■ Dark olive green bead
- ■ Medium green bead
- □ Yellow green bead
- □ Yellow bead
- ■ Golden orange bead
- ■ Orange bead
- ■ Red bead

Slide the indicated colored bead into the stitch with a plaited knit stitch on the right side and a purl stitch on the wrong side.

CHART A

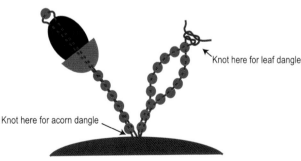

Knot here for leaf dangle

Knot here for acorn dangle

FIGURE 1

OCEAN-SPIRALS HAT

This is a great project for practicing your new bead knitting skills, and you get a funky hat with an oceany spray of beads in the bargain.

Bead
Knitting

SKILL LEVEL
INTERMEDIATE

INSTRUCTIONS

Beginning at Hat Brim
String all the beads onto the yarn.

Cast on 122 sts.

Row 1: K1, (p3, plk3, p3, plk3, p3, plk9) repeat 5 times, k1.
Row 2: K1, (k3, p3, k3, p3, k3, p9) repeat 5 times, k1.
Row 3: Repeat row 1.
Rows 4-15: Following chart A, knit patterns D, C, D, B, D, A, D, B, or arrange in your choice of pattern for the bead sections, separated by the rib pattern D, and knitting the first and last st of ea row creating a selvage for sewing the seam.
Rows 16–18: Repeat rows 1–3.
K3, p3 for 3 in (7.5 cm). Beginning next row on the beadwork side of the hat, dec 1 st on ea knit rib (102 sts). Next row k the knit sts and p the purl sts. Next row, dec 1 st on ea knit rib (82 sts). Next 2 rows, k the knit sts and p the purl sts. Next row dec ea purl st so that the hat is all st st (62 sts). Knit 2 rows st st, then (k2, k2tog) across the row, k the last 2 sts (47 sts). Repeat the last 3 rows (36 sts). Purl the next row. K1, k2tog across the next row (24 sts). Repeat the last 2 rows 3 times (16 sts, then 11 sts, 8 sts). Weave tail through remaining stitches and sew seam.

SIZE
To fit head circumference 20 to 22 in (51 to 56 cm).

FINISHED KNITTED MEASUREMENTS
From center top of hat to brim: 10 in (25.5 cm)
Circumference of brim: 20 in (51 cm)

MATERIALS
Approx. 210 yd (130 m) worsted-weight yarn
160 size 5 light-blue triangle beads
Size 7 (4.5 mm) needles, or size to obtain gauge
Size 10 beading needle
Sewing thread
Tapestry needle for sewing seams together

GAUGE IN PLAITED STOCKINETTE STITCH VARIATION
5 sts = 1 in (2.5 cm)
7 rows = 1 in (2.5 cm)

The sample project was made using 1 skein each of Kureyon 100% wool, 108 yd (100 m), 1.75 oz (50 gr) per skein, color #13 and #40 by Eisaku Noro.

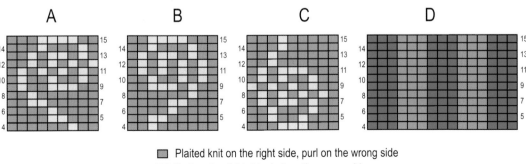

CHART A

- ▨ Plaited knit on the right side, purl on the wrong side
- ▦ Purl on the right side, knit on the wrong side
- ☐ Push a bead into the stitch, plaited knitting on the right side, purling on the wrong side

FLORAL-PANEL SWEATER

Bead
Knitting

SKILL LEVEL
INTERMEDIATE

This sweater, with its center bead knitted panel, is actually easier to knit than the Autumn Leaves Beret. By filling in the background stitches of the center panel with smaller size 8 seed beads, you not only save the center knitting from being too heavy with beads, but once the tedious part of stringing the beads onto the yarn is complete, you get to relax by just knitting back and forth. You don't have to make decisions about where to knit the beads since you knit a bead into every stitch except the two stitches at each side.

INSTRUCTIONS

Back
Using size 6 (5.25 mm) needles, cast on 88 (92, 96, 100, 108) sts.

Rows 1 and 2: (K2, p2) repeat across.
Rows 3 and 4: (P2, k2) repeat across.

Repeat these 4 rows again, then work in st st until piece measures 26 in (40.5 cm). Bind off.

Front Side Panels
Using the size 6 (5.25 mm) needles, cast on 32 (36, 36, 40, 40) sts. Work the same as for the back until piece measures 22 in (56 cm). On the center side, dec 1 st every row 8 (10, 10, 10, 10) times, 22 (26, 26, 30, 30) sts. Knit in st st for 1½ in (4 cm), place rem sts on st holder.

Repeat for other front side panel, decreasing on the opposite side.

SIZES
To fit chest sizes 34 in (36, 38, 40, 42 in), (86.5, 91.5, 96.5, 101.5, 106.5 cm). Instructions are for the smallest size, with larger sizes in parentheses. If there are no parentheses, the number is for all sizes.

FINISHED KNITTED MEASUREMENTS
Bust: 36 in (38, 40, 42, 44 in), (91.5, 96.5, 101.5, 106.5, 111.5 cm)
Length: 26 in (66 cm)
Upper Arm: 17½ in (17½, 18, 18, 18½ in), (33.5, 33.5, 45.5, 45.5, 47 cm)

MATERIALS
13 (14, 14, 15, 16) 135 yd (125 m) skeins of worsted-weight yarn
Approx. 100 gr of blue size 8 seed beads that fit on the yarn
Approx. 50 gr of pearl cream size 6 seed beads that fit on the yarn
Approx. 50 gr of green size 6 seed beads that fit on the yarn
Approx. 10 gr or less of the other size 6 beads in colors shown on chart A
Size 6 (5.25 mm) needles, or size to obtain gauge
Size 5 (5 mm) needles
Needle to string beads onto yarn
Tapestry needle for sewing together seams

GAUGE IN STOCKINETTE STITCH USING SIZE 6 NEEDLES
19 sts = 4 in (10 cm)
29 rows = 4 in (10 cm)

Sleeves

Using the size 6 (5.25 mm) needles, cast on 44 (44, 48, 48, 52) sts. Work the same as the back for the first 8 rows. Continue in st st, increasing 1 st at each side every sixth row, 19 times, 82 (82, 86, 86, 90) sts. Work even until sleeve measures 18 in (18½, 19, 19½, 19½ in), (45.5, 47, 48.5, 49.5, 49.5 cm). Bind off.

Center Front Bead Knitted Panel

String the beads, following chart A, graph 1, working from left to right, then right to left, row by row from the top to the bottom. Repeat on a separate skein of yarn, then string beads as shown in graph 2 on a third skein of yarn. Using the size 5 (5 mm) needles, and 1 of the bead strung skeins of yarn from graph 1, cast on 32 sts. Work the same as the back for the first 8 rows. Work in plaited st st variation, knitting the first and last 2 stitches without beads, and all the other stitches with beads. Change to the bead-strung skein of yarn from graph 2 when you have finished knitting all the beads from the first skein. Repeat for the last skein. Work in k2, p2 rib until piece measures 22 in (56 cm). Move sts to holder.

Assembly

Stitch the front side panels to the center bead panel. Stitch the front and back shoulder seams together. Center the sleeves over the shoulder seam and stitch in place. Sew the sleeve seams and front to back side seams.

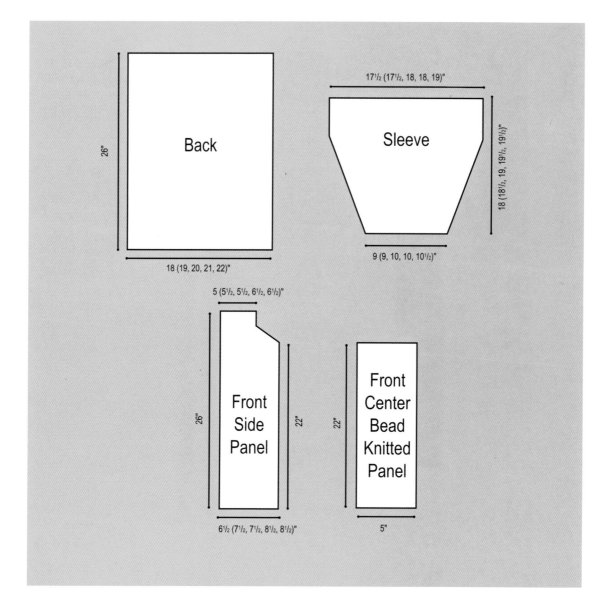

Collar

Using the size 5 (5.5 mm) needles pick up the 32 sts from the center bead knitted panel, 16 sts from ea of the front side panels, and 32, (32, 35, 35, 35) sts along the back neckline. Continuing k2, p2 rib pattern on front panel, work k2, p2 rib around until collar measures 2½ in (6.5 cm). Bind off loosely.

This project was made using 15 skeins of Jaeger Handknit's Extra Fine Merino, 100% extra fine merino wool, 1.75 oz (50 g), 135 yd (125 m), color #946 Blueberry.

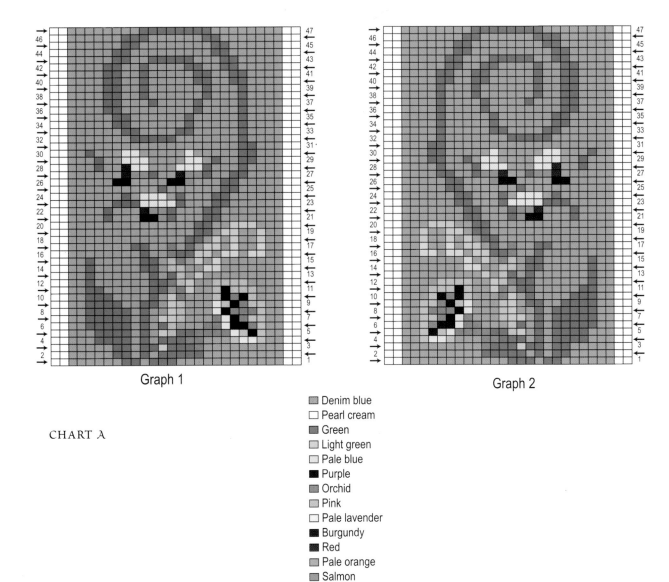

Graph 1

Graph 2

CHART A

- ▨ Denim blue
- ☐ Pearl cream
- ▨ Green
- ☐ Light green
- ☐ Pale blue
- ■ Purple
- ▨ Orchid
- ▨ Pink
- ☐ Pale lavender
- ■ Burgundy
- ▨ Red
- ▨ Pale orange
- ▨ Salmon
- ☐ Pale peach

PULLING IT ALL TOGETHER

The creative possibilities for knitting with beads increase exponentially when you start combining techniques. For instance, you can pre-string beads and knit them into your garment, then add a fringe or embroider a pattern as well. The Black Diamond Hat has a touch of beaded knitting at its cuff and a group of fringe dangles at the tip. The Falling Leaves Scarf is made with single color bead knitting plus an elegant two-layer fringe. The Delicate Lace Scarf employs sparkly crystals and size 8 seed beads in beaded knit diamonds, and then adds a delicate pearl and crystal fringe. The casual Striped Blouse is made using both beaded knitting and beads over slip stitch. Finally, the Black Evening Camisole uses an all-over pattern of beaded knitting and ends with a bead netted fringe. Be sure to look back to the basic steps in the previous sections for helpful information on unfamiliar techniques.

BLACK-DIAMOND HAT

Simple and quick to make, this funky hat with its long tail is a great beginning project for knitting with beads. Make it red or green with white beads to wear during the holidays and you'll feel like one of Santa's elves.

INSTRUCTIONS

String the hexagonal beads onto the yarn. Cast on 98 sts. Follow the line-by-line instructions below, or the pattern in chart A, through Row 7.

Row 1: (p2, k2) repeat to the last 2 sts, p2.

Row 2: K the knit sts, and p the purl sts.

Row 3: (p2, k2, p1, B1, p1, k2) repeat to the last 2 sts, p2.

Row 4: (k2, p2, k1, B2, k1, p2) repeat to the last 2 sts, k2.

Row 5: (p2, k2, p1, B3, p1, k2) repeat to the last 2 sts, p2.

Row 6: (k2, p2, k1, B2, k1, p2) repeat to the last 2 sts, k2.

Row 7: (p2, k2, p1, B1, p1, k2) repeat to the last 2 sts, p2.

Repeat Row 2 until the hat is 7½ in (19 cm) long. Dec 1 st at each end every 4 rows, until there are 36 sts left. Cut the yarn to 24 in (61 cm) and weave through the rem sts. Sew side seam. Weave in ends.

Beadwork Tassel

Attach an 8-ft (2.4 m) length of beading thread to the point of the hat. String the large accent bead, then make a dangle by stringing the beads as shown in figure 1, passing back through all the beads except the last 3 beads strung. Pass the thread through the yarn at the point of the hat and then back through the large bead. Make about 12 dangles in the same way, and then anchor the thread in the tail of the hat and weave in the end.

This project was made using 4 skeins of Berroco's Sensuwool, 80% wool/20% nylon, 1.75 oz (50 g), 90 yd (83 m,), color #6334 black.

SIZES

To fit 20- to 22-in (51- to 56-cm) circumference head

FINISHED KNITTED MEASUREMENTS

14 in (35.5 cm) circumference, unstretched
About 27 in (68 cm) long, from end to end

MATERIALS

Approx. 270 yd (250 m) of worsted-weight yarn
108 hexagonal beads large enough to string onto the yarn
1 oz (28 gr) of size 11 seed beads
¼ oz (7 gr) of size 8 seed beads
1 large accent bead
12 size 5 or size 6 round beads
12 small drop beads
Size 8 (5 mm) needles, or size to obtain gauge
Needle to string beads onto yarn
Size 11 beading needle
Beading thread
Tapestry needle for sewing seams together

GAUGE IN STOCKINETTE STITCH

18 sts = 4 in (10 cm)
26 rows = 4 in (10 cm)

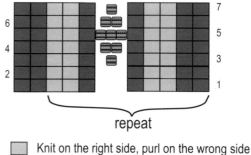

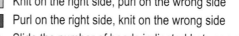

repeat

Knit on the right side, purl on the wrong side
Purl on the right side, knit on the wrong side
 Slide the number of beads indicated between stitches

CHART A

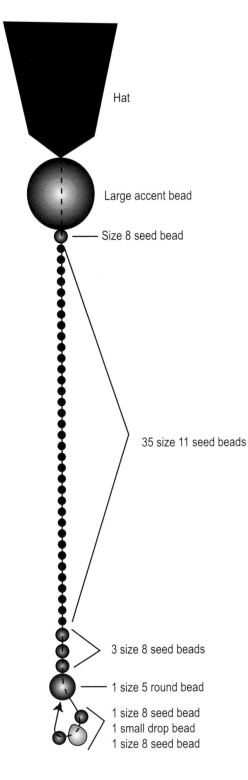

Hat

Large accent bead

Size 8 seed bead

35 size 11 seed beads

3 size 8 seed beads

1 size 5 round bead

1 size 8 seed bead
1 small drop bead
1 size 8 seed bead

FIGURE 1

FALLING-LEAVES SCARF

This elegant scarf is the perfect accessory for a chilly fall day. The subtle coloring of the hand-dyed yarn plays nicely off the rich bronze tones of the beadwork pattern. And the fringe with the leaf beads continues the autumn theme.

FINISHED KNITTED MEASUREMENTS
52 x 8 in (132 x 20.5 cm) including fringe

MATERIALS
Approx. 300 yd (270 m) dk weight yarn
Approx. 3 oz (84 gr) of size 5 seed beads in bronze
A variety of beads for the fringe as indicated on the fringe figure
Size 6 (4 mm) needles, or size to obtain gauge
Size 10 beading needle
Stitch holder
Beading thread
Tapestry needle for grafting sections together

GAUGE IN PLAITED STOCKINETTE STITCH VARIATION
21 sts = 4 in (10 cm)
24 rows = 4 in (10 cm)

INSTRUCTIONS
Scarf
String half the size 5 bronze beads onto the yarn.

Cast on 5 sts. Follow the leaf pattern chart A, sliding a bead into place where indicated on the pattern. Repeat row 47 until the piece measures 23 in (58 cm), or one-half the desired length, less the fringe. Move stitches to a stitch holder. String the rest of the beads onto the skein of yarn and make the other end of the scarf in the same way. Graft the two pieces of knitting together.

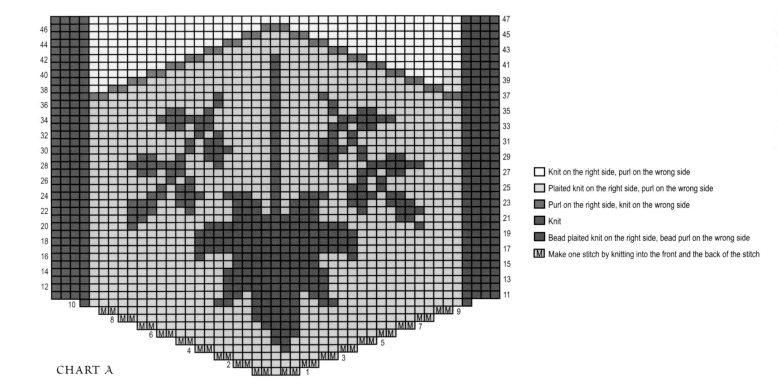

CHART A

- ☐ Knit on the right side, purl on the wrong side
- ☐ Plaited knit on the right side, purl on the wrong side
- ▨ Purl on the right side, knit on the wrong side
- ▨ Knit
- ▨ Bead plaited knit on the right side, bead purl on the wrong side
- Ⓜ Make one stitch by knitting into the front and the back of the stitch

Fringe

Use the beading thread and beading needle to stitch the fringe on the edge of each end of the scarf. Begin by stitching the back row of fringe in figure 1, repeating section A 10 times along the scarf edge, then ending with section B. Make the top beadwork detail by first stringing the large leaf and bead sections, passing in and out of the size 8 beads from the back fringe, as shown in figure 2, step 1. Finally, stitch the line of size 11 bronze beads along the scarf edge, as shown in step 2 in figure 2. Tack down the bronze bead picots by passing back through the top bead, and then stitching through the knitting. Weave in ends. Repeat for the other end of the scarf.

The sample project was made using 1 skein of Kathleen Hughes Hand Dyed Originals, 55% mohair/45% merino wool, 8 oz (224 gr), 488 yd (450 m), color #209.

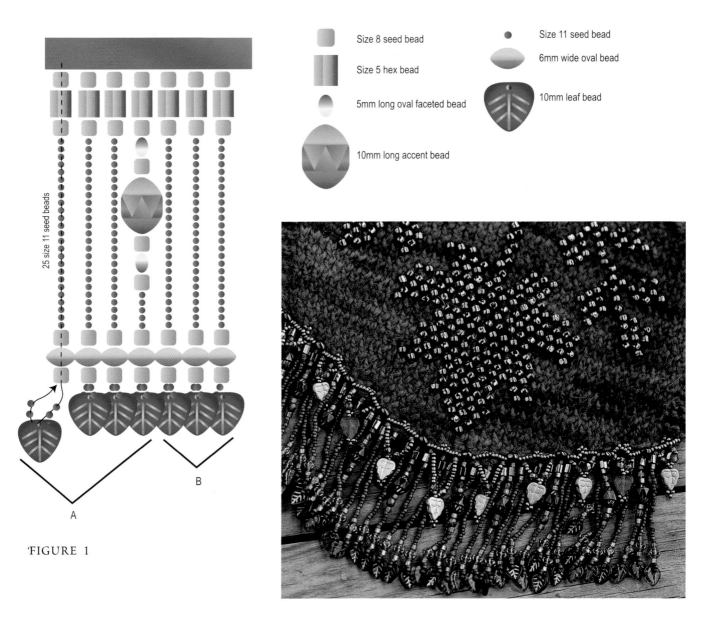

25 size 11 seed beads

Size 8 seed bead

Size 5 hex bead

5mm long oval faceted bead

10mm long accent bead

Size 11 seed bead

6mm wide oval bead

10mm leaf bead

A

B

FIGURE 1

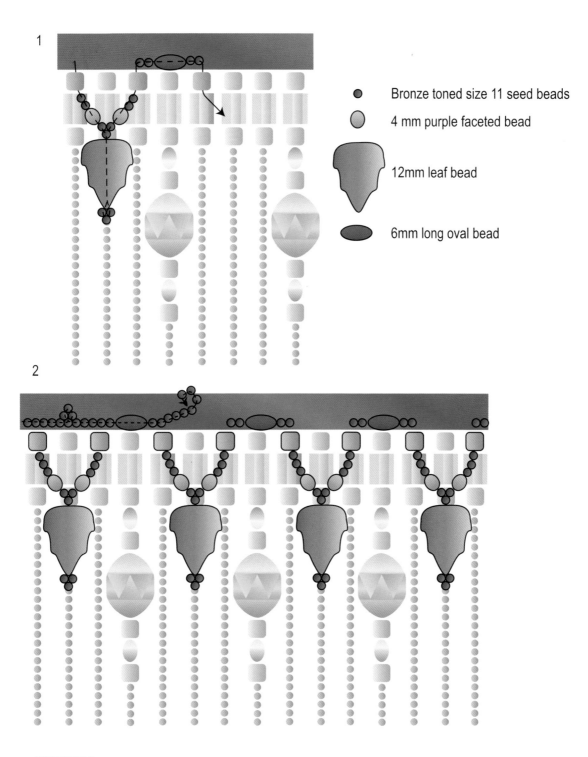

1

2

Bronze toned size 11 seed beads

4 mm purple faceted bead

12mm leaf bead

6mm long oval bead

FIGURE 2

DELICATE LACE SCARF

Making this delicate piece is like learning to do two scarves in one lesson. The three-point beginning, with the pre-strung bead knitting and diamond pattern lacework, switches over to a simple open-work pattern with an easy bead-embroidered fringe. Make it as shown or fashion a whole scarf with one or the other pattern.

FINISHED KNITTED MEASUREMENTS
55 x 10 in (139.5 x 25.5 cm), including fringe

MATERIALS
Approx. 250 yd (230 m) of lace weight yarn
175 clear Swarovski crystals, 4mm in size
225 pearl-toned size 8 seed beads
Fringe beads: 4 gr size 11 clear seed beads, 4 gr size 8 white seed beads,
    4 gr size 15 white seed beads, 18 Swarovski crystals, 4mm in size,
    18 pearls, 6mm in size
Size 4 (3.5 mm) needles or size to obtain gauge
Needle to thread beads onto yarn
Beading needle and thread for fringe

GAUGE IN STOCKINETTE STITCH
24 sts = 4 in (10 cm)
38 rows = 4 in (10 cm)

INSTRUCTIONS
Use the adjacent pre-stringing guide to string the beads onto the yarn before beginning the first half of the scarf.

White Lace Scarf Pre-Stringing Guide
✧ - 4mm Swarovski Crystal
□ - Size 8 seed bead

String each column, top to bottom, beginning with the left column and working to the right.

34 ✧	4 ✧	2 ✧	1 ✧
1 □	6 □	9 □	9 □
4 ✧	4 ✧	1 ✧	3 ✧
1 □	5 □	10 □	6 □
4 ✧	4 ✧	1 ✧	4 ✧
1 □	5 □	10 □	6 □
4 ✧	4 ✧	1 ✧	4 ✧
3 □	8 □	5 □	6 □
4 ✧	4 ✧	2 ✧	3 ✧
2 □	6 □	8 □	5 □
4 ✧	4 ✧	2 ✧	2 ✧
2 □	6 □	8 □	5 □
	4 ✧	2 ✧	2 ✧
	9 □	8 □	5 □
	3 ✧	3 ✧	1 ✧
	9 □	9 □	
	3 ✧	1 ✧	
	9 □	9 □	
	3 ✧		
	9 □		
	2 ✧		
	8 □		
	2 ✧		
	8 □		

Individual point of scarf—string pattern three times.

2 ✧
2 □
3 ✧
1 □
10 ✧

Following chart A, knit the first point of the scarf. Break the yarn leaving a 4-in (10-cm) tail and leave the knitting on the needle. Repeat chart A, making another point and slide it next to the first, breaking the yarn and leaving a 4-in (10-cm) tail. Repeat once more, but don't break the yarn. You will have three points on one needle.

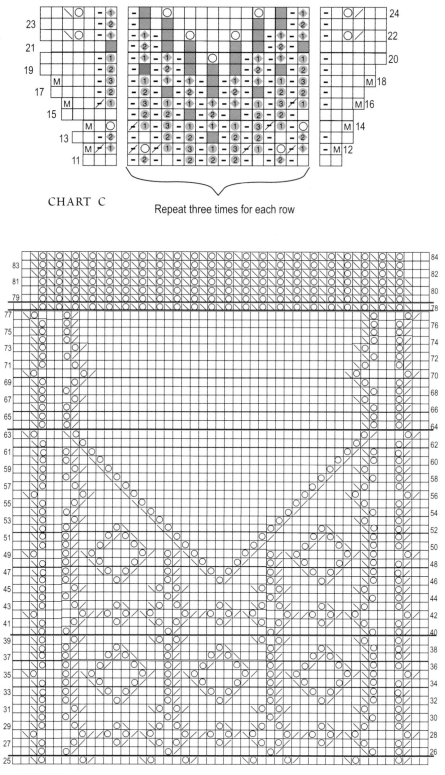

CHART C

Repeat three times for each row

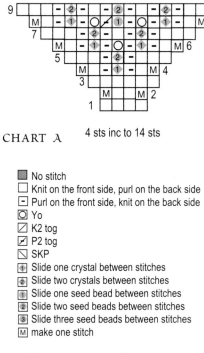

CHART A

4 sts inc to 14 sts

■ No stitch
□ Knit on the front side, purl on the back side
– Purl on the front side, knit on the back side
O Yo
⟋ K2 tog
⟍ P2 tog
◣ SKP
① Slide one crystal between stitches
② Slide two crystals between stitches
❶ Slide one seed bead between stitches
❷ Slide two seed beads between stitches
❸ Slide three seed beads between stitches
Ⓜ make one stitch

Follow row 10 on chart B, using the working yarn and knitting across all 3 points, joining them together.

Follow row 11 through 24 on chart C, working each side once and the center section 3 times.

Follow chart D for the lace pattern on the scarf, working rows 25 through 39, then repeating rows 26 through 39, then working rows 40 through 77, then repeating rows 64 through 77. Work row 78, then

CHART D

CHART B

repeat rows 79 through 84 until the scarf measures approximately 52 in (132 cm) long. Work in st st for 5 rows. Bind off very loosely. Block, stretching with pins placed in edge holes to pull sides into scallops along sides of scarf.

Following the design pattern in figure 1, stitch the fringe beads onto the ends of the scarf.

This project was made using 1 skein Crystal Palace's Lace Yarn, 100% wool, 3.5 oz (100 g), 848 yd (775 m), color #57 natural.

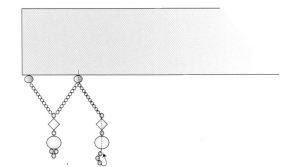

FIGURE 1

- ◦ Size 15 seed bead
- ◦ Size 11 seed bead
- ◦ Size 8 seed bead
- ◇ 4mm crystal
- ◯ 6mm pearl

STRIPED BLOUSE

A fun-to-knit design, this blouse combines simple stripes, eyelets, and beads to create a lot of detail with minimal effort. The bead techniques are from the sections on Beads Over Slip Stitch and Beaded Knitting, where beads are simply slid between stitches or held in front of the knitting while stitches are slipped behind.

SIZES

To fit chest sizes 34 in (36, 38, 40, 42 in),. (86.5, 91.5, 96.5, 101.5, 106.5 cm). Instructions are for the smallest size, with larger sizes in parentheses. If there are no parentheses, the number is for all sizes.

FINISHED KNITTED MEASUREMENTS

Bust: 38 in (40, 42, 44, 46 in), (96.5, 101.5, 106.5, 111.5, 117 cm)
Front Length: 16 in (16½, 17, 17½, 18 in), (40.5, 412, 43, 44.5, 45.5 cm)
Upper Arm: 17 in(17½, 18, 18½, 19 in). (43, 44.5, 45.5, 47, 48.5 cm)

MATERIALS

3 (3, 3, 3, 4) 256 yd (233 m) skeins of sport-weight yarn in taupe
Two 108 yd (100 m) skeins each of pale green, light gray, and beige sport-weight yarn
Approx. ¾ oz (20 gr) size 6 seed beads
Size 6 (4 mm) needles or size to obtain gauge
Needle to string bead onto yarn
Tapestry needle for sewing together seams

GAUGE IN STOCKINETTE STITCH

20 sts = 4 in (10 cm)
24 rows = 4 in (10 cm)

INSTRUCTIONS

Back

Beginning at the top of the blouse, using the taupe yarn, cast on 95 (100, 105, 110, 115) sts. Knit in st st for 16¾ in (17¼, 17¾, 18¼, 18¾ in), (42.5, 43.5, 45, 46.5, 47.5 cm). On the next right side row, work (k3, yo, k2tog) repeat across the row, knitting the extra sts at the end of the row. Work in st st for 4 more rows. Bind off.

Front

String 24 in (61 cm) of beads onto 1 skein ea of the gray and beige yarn. Set aside. Beginning at the top of the blouse, using the taupe yarn, cast on 95 (100, 105, 110, 115) sts. Knit in st st for 3 in (7.5 cm), and then work chart A, repeating the pattern across knitting with a partial repeat at the end of the row, as necessary. Work in st st for 4 in (4½, 5, 5½, 6 in), (10, 11.5, 12.5, 14, 15 cm), then work pattern in chart B, repeating the pattern across knitting with a partial repeat at the end of the row, as necessary. Bind off.

Sleeves

String 12 in (30.5 cm) of beads onto 1 skein ea of the gray and beige yarn. Set aside. Using the taupe yarn, cast on 85 (88, 90, 93, 95) sts. Knit in st st for 2 in (5 cm), and then work chart A through line 21. Work in st st for 2 in (2¼, 2½, 2¾, 3 in), (5, 5.5, 6.5, 7, 7.5 cm). At the same time, after the first 8 rows of knitting, decrease 1 st ea side every right side row 20 times. Work pattern in chart B from line 18 through line 27, repeating the pattern across knitting with a partial repeat at the end of the row, as necessary. Bind off.

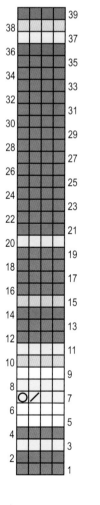

CHART A

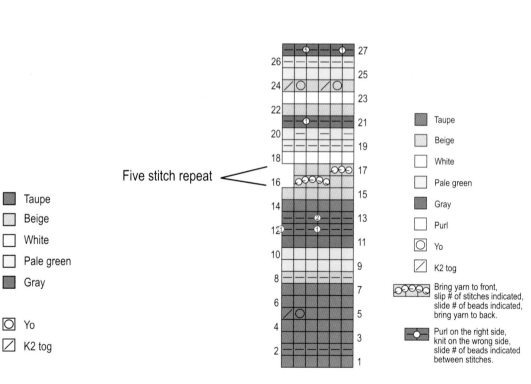

Five stitch repeat

CHART B

Legend:
- Taupe
- Beige
- White
- Pale green
- Gray
- Purl
- ◎ Yo
- ⊘ K2 tog
- ○○○○ Bring yarn to front, slip # of stitches indicated, slide # of beads indicated, bring yarn to back.
- Purl on the right side, knit on the wrong side, slide # of beads indicated between stitches.

Chart A legend:
- Taupe
- Beige
- White
- Pale green
- Gray
- ◎ Yo
- ⊘ K2 tog

Assembly

Do not block. Steam press all but the top front and back. Fold up the back bottom edge along the picot and stitch in place. Sew front and back tog at shoulders. Center sleeve over shoulder seam and sew in place. Sew side seams of sleeve and blouse. Weave in ends.

This project was made using Tahki Yarn's Cotton Classic, 100% mercerized cotton, 1.75 oz (50 g), 108 yd (100 m), 2 skeins ea of #3211 mushroom, #3752 dusty green, #3066 green ice, #3034 gray; and 3 skeins of Classic Elite's Provence, 100% mercerized Egyptian cotton, 4.4 oz (125 g), 256 yd (233 m) in #2645 linen.

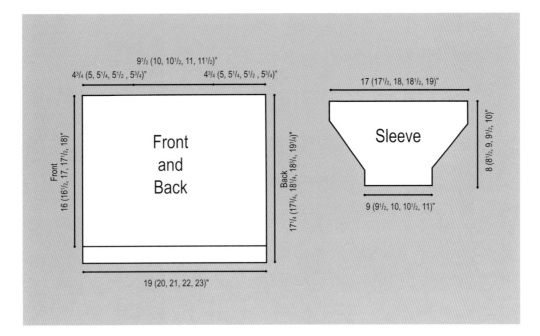

BLACK EVENING CAMISOLE

An opulent camisole for a fabulous evening out, this loose fitting top is embellished with scattered, smoky, silver-toned beads and a swaying fringe at the hem. The beads are easy to knit into the fabric.

INSTRUCTIONS

Body

Before beginning knitting, string 125 of the size 6 beads onto 1 skein of yarn. Use this skein for beginning the body. As you are knitting, and you get near the end of the skein of yarn, add more beads from that end, if you need them, or slide off the extra beads, if necessary. Before beginning the next skein of yarn, note how many beads you used on the first. That will be how many you need to string on the second skein before attaching it. Repeat for each skein as you work.

Using size 8 (5 mm) circular needle, cast on 154 (160, 172, 184, 190) sts. Join into a circle. Place marker. This marks the front just before the cable detail.

Row 1: (P1, B1, p1) repeat around.
Rows 2–5: Work in st st.
Row 6: P2, k2, p2, k8, p2, k2, p2, (p1, B1, p1, k4) repeat to last 2 sts in row, p1, B1, p1.
Rows 7–10: P the purl sts, k the knit sts of the first 20 sts, work in st st for the rem sts.
Row 11: P2, k2, p2, next 2 sts to holder in back, k2, k2 from holder, next 2 sts to holder in front, k2, k2 from holder, p2, k2 p2, k3 (p1, B1, p1, k4) repeat to last 5 sts, p1, B1, p1, k3.
Rows 12–15: Repeat rows 7–10.

SIZES

To fit chest sizes 34 in (36, 38, 40, 42 in), (86.5, 91.5, 96.5, 101.5, 106.5 cm). Instructions are for the smallest size, with larger sizes in parentheses. If there are no parentheses, the number is for all sizes.

FINISHED KNITTED MEASUREMENTS

Bust: 34 in (36, 38, 40, 42 in), (86.5, 91.5, 96.5, 101.5, 106.5 cm)
Length, not including straps and fringe: 11½ in (29 cm)
Straps: 9 in (23 cm)

MATERIALS

4 (5, 5, 6, 6) 90 yd (83 m) skeins of worsted weight yarn
Approx. 3 oz (85 gr) of size 6 steel-colored seed beads
Approx. 3 oz (85 gr) of size 11 steel-colored seed beads
Approx. 50 ½-in-long (1.3 cm) dagger drop beads
Size 8 (5 mm) circular needle, or size to obtain gauge
Size 7 (4.5 mm) needles
Size 10 beading needle
Beading thread
Tapestry needle for sewing seams together

GAUGE IN STOCKINETTE STITCH

18 sts = 4 in (10 cm)
24 rows = 4 in (10 cm)

Next 3 rows: Purl the p sts, knit the k sts.

Next row: (P1, B1, p1) repeat around. Bind off.

Right Strap

String 72 size 6 beads.

Using size 7 (4.5 mm) needles, cast on 10 sts.

Row 1: Knit.
Row 2: K3, p4, k3.
Row 3: Knit.
Row 4: K2, B1, k1, p4, k1, B1, k2.
Row 5: K3, 2 sts to st holder in front, k2, k2 from st holder, k3
Rows 6, 8 and 10: Repeat row 4
Rows 7 and 9: Knit.
Row 11: Repeat row 5
Repeat row 6 through row 11 ten times (12 twisted cables)
Repeat row 4 and row 3 twice.
Repeat row 2.
Bind off.

Left Strap

Work the same as for the right strap, except on row 5, move sts on st holder to the back of the work, instead of the front.

Sew straps to body, 4 in (10 cm) from center front and center back.

Beaded Fringe

Follow the fringe pattern in figure 1, stitching the fringe to the beads knitted into the first row of the body.

The sample project was made using 5 skeins of Sensuwool, 80% wool/20% nylon, 90 yd (83 m), 1.75 oz (50 gr) per skein, color #6334 black by Berroco.

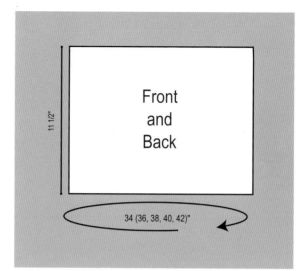

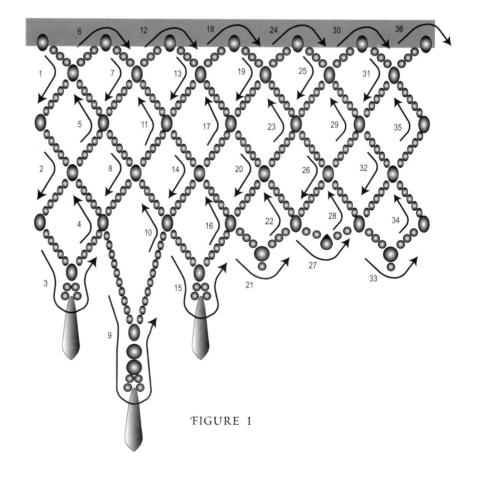

FIGURE 1

BIBLIOGRAPHY

There aren't many sources for knitting with beads using yarn other than single projects here and there in magazines and books. Here are some publications I have been involved with, or that I have used for information and inspiration.

Davis, Jane. *The Complete Guide to Beading Techniques,* Iola, WI: Krause Publishing, 2001
– This book covers over a dozen beadwork techniques and has 30 projects, including three for knitting with beads.

Gourley, Elizabeth, Jane Davis and Ellen Talbott. *Art of Seed Beading,* New York: Sterling Publishing, 1999.
– On pages 90 and 94 of this book are a cotton cord and size 8 bead knitted jewelry bag, using size 2 knitting needles and a small purse, knit in size 000 needles and size 11 beads.

Haertig, Evelyn. *More Beautiful Purses.* Carmel, CA: Gallery Graphics Press, 1990.
– This is a fabulous book on purses that were made 100 years ago and earlier. There are many bead knitted purses and bags.

Korach, Alice. "Knitted Bead Purses," *Bead & Button,* No. 2 (April 1994): 22-23. "Bead-Knitting Madness," *Threads Magazine,* No. 24 (Aug/Sept 1989): 24-29.
– Alice Korach, editor of *Bead and Button,* describes in detail her method of bead knitting, which is the technique I use in the section called Bead Knitting.

Schurenberg, Sabina. *Glasperlarbeiten Taschen und Beutel.* Munchen: Hirmer, 1998.
– This is another fabulous book that focuses on antique bead knitted purses and bags. The fact that it is written in German doesn't diminish its value for those who don't read German, as it is filled with full-color photos and color-charted patterns of the designs (though they are a bit small).

Williams, Theresa. *The Bag Lady Series.*
Box 2409
Evergreen, CO 80437-2409
1 (888) 222-4523
www.baglady.com.
– This is a series of six self-published books on beaded knitted purses, and also a source of mail-order supplies for projects listed in the books.

ACKNOWLEDGEMENTS

Thank you **Ronni Lundy**, my wonderful editor, for your patience, understanding, and final help on pulling this book together.

Thank you **Mailyn Hastings** for your wise technical consultation and unstinting attention to detail at the copyediting stage.

Thank you **Katherine Aimone** for your humor and patience throughout the seemingly never-ending process of writing this book.

Thank you **Valerie Shrader** for your help and suggestions at the editing stage.

Thank you to **Wright Creative Photography & Design**, photographer **Sandra Stambaugh**, art directors **Celia Naranjo, Tom Metcalf, and Chris Bryant** for creating such fabulous photographs.

Thank you **Carol Taylor** for the opportunity to write this book.

Thank you to all the yarn companies whose fabulous yarns inspired many of the projects in this book:
Baabajoes
Berroco
Brown Sheep
Classic Elite
Dale of Norway
Knit One Crochet Too
Plymouth Yarn
Reynolds Yarns
Rowan Yarns
Tahki Yarns

INDEX

A Note About Suppliers
Usually, the supplies you need for making the projects in Lark books can be found at your local craft supply store, discount mart, home improvement center, or retail shop relevant to the topic of the book. Occasionally, however, you may need to buy materials or tools from specialty suppliers. In order to provide you with the most up-to-date information, we have created a listing of suppliers on our Web site, which we update on a regular basis. Visit us at www.larkbooks.com, click on "Craft Supply Sources," and then click on the relevant topic. You will find numerous companies listed with their web address and/or mailing address and phone number.